IN QUEST OF DAIBUL

IN QUEST OF DAIBUL
AND OTHER SPEECHES

MUMTAZ HASAN

Foreword by
PROFESSOR G. TUCCI

Published by
THE WRITERS' GUILD, KARACHI

Published by United Advertisers for the Writers' Guild, Karachi and
Printed at Vision Publications Limited., Karachi.

CONTENTS

FOREWORD

It is a great honour for me to preface this book by Mr. Mumtaz Hasan because it is always an honour to be associated with the intellectual achievements or be familiar with the thought of outstanding personalities. And Mr. Mumtaz Hasan is indeed an outstanding personality for his proficiency in so many and different activities and interests which he blends in a living and most active harmony. Of course you cannot speak of a man if you do not know him personally; if you were to judge him only by his writings or from hearsay, your opinion about him would be imperfect, superficial, even misleading. You must know a man as he is, in his daily life, have especially the privilege of discussion with him, because only through dialogue and conversation can you establish with him that intellectual and spiritual correspondence which opens to us the mind and soul of our friends. I am fortunate enough in having had many contacts and exchanges of ideas with Mr. Mumtaz Hasan. If I well remember, our first meeting took place in Bhambore where Dr. F. A. Khan, Director of Archaeology in Pakistan, had started his famous excavations. I then realized that I was confronted not only with a great authority on banking, economy and finance, but also with a man who knows the history of Pakistan as few others do. Being in a position to do it, he greatly encouraged and supported archaeological enterprises, with the purpose of throwing light upon many dark points of the history of Pakistan. I say that he was in a position to do it, on account of his very high office in the State administration. But how many persons in other countries, having the same authority, take an equal interest in archaeology or in history? The fact is that Mumtaz Hasan is what we term a humanist, a man of wide intellectual interests and of great learning, open to all sorts of problems and for whom there is no human endeavour, past or present, no field of science, no research, which does not awaken the alertness of his spirit.

The humanistic approach is becoming a rare plant in the barrenness of present-day life, in which only the dryness of things practical and immediately profitable, or the uncertain and ever-changing winds of politics, seem to lay waste the noblest aspirations of man. There is no doubt that when writing the cultural history of present-day Pakistan, one must make a large place for Mumtaz Hasan: be it as a patron of archaeological and historical researches, as a sponsor of literary activities, as a promoter of Urdu studies, or as a most active inspirer of the cultural collaboration between Pakistan and other nations.

In saying this, I am not prompted by partiality, nor by uncritical admiration for a friend. The present book itself, in which one can realize the wide range of the author's cultural interests, bears out my words : his mastery of Urdu, Arabic, and Persian literatures, attested by the most appropriate quotations, springing from a never-exhausted source, that intersperse his prose, as well as his command of English. Reading the following pages you can realize how the problems which he discusses acquire from the touch of his pen a lively, actual incisiveness. This is a rather rare quality in writing, which either soars in the remote atmosphere of abstractions or stifles whatever inspiration there is in the dryness of facts and statements. Mumtaz Hasan is a writer because he is alert and alive to all sorts of problems, he feels them as a part of himself, as his best self. I remember when, as Vice-President of the Iqbal Academy he spoke in Turin, where I had asked him to speak on Iqbal the Poet, with whom I had the privilege of being personally acquainted and whom I met in Lahore. I remember, I say, how humanly he spoke of the great poet : not only did he recall the art of Iqbal, but his approach to the subject was so sensitive and sympathetic, that we could almost see Muhammad Iqbal present among us.

What he writes about museums is worthy of meditation : museums are not intended for scholars only, they are the best way of conveying to common people the everlasting documents of national traditions in their never-ceasing progress through the alternating moments of heroic achievements or passing doubts of joyful and blessed creatures. We fully agree with him on this matter, and wish that in every country this peculiar reflex of a culture be multiplied for the benefit of all. Museums, built on the various sites of archaeological, artistic and historical interest, are likely to become a focus of attraction for everybody; nationals as well as foreigners, chiefly the latter, because I am certain that in a few years Asia will arouse the ever-increasing interest of tourists. We have made too much of Europe, of which we now know almost every corner, and we wish to be better acquainted with new landscapes, new documents of art, far more than we have been so far. And here the man interested in the economic development of his country, who is Mr.

Mumtaz Hasan, will join the humanist and the historian.

I have read with equal interest his lecture on writers : perhaps never before have writers enjoyed such a prominent place in society. This implies a greater, an immense responsibility for them, because now that culture is no longer the privilege of a few educated people but is a common heritage in which large masses are partaking, the influence exerted by writers, the inspiration which man can draw from them, is spreading on a large, unprecedented scale. Unfortunately, there are signs that writers do not always follow their free inspiration, do not intend to educate people, to introduce them to the cult of that which is good and beautiful, but are rather bent on following the general trends which are not always the best.

It thus happens that forsaking their role of educating through their original and deeply felt ideals, they are merely imitators of fashion : this may be rewarding, may even bestow on a writer a fleeting fame, but we should keep in mind that fashions are short-lived ; and that the greatest geniuses, rather than complying with the common ways of thought or expression, have always opened up new avenues and proposed new ideas, independently and freely. It seems to me that the greatness of a writer is to be measured by the peculiar features of his art and the contents of his works.

Above all, art should be independent of politics, because the realm of beauty transcends the ephemeral, ever-changing demands and tides of history. It no doubt reflects the feelings and aspirations of a time, but it purifies them in the clarity of a passionless aloofness.

But I do not want to spend any more words in prefacing this fine book : it speaks for itself and the Author is so well-known that any praise whatever would be hardly appropriate. Nobody praises a mountain because it is high, or the sea because it is deep. I only wish that the example set by Mumtaz Hasan may have many imitators among influential men, and not only in Pakistan, and that his initiative may continue for a long time to benefit humanistic studies and to strengthen the cultural ties among nations.

Rome,   **G. Tucci**

April, 1966

PREFACE

If there is one man who is responsible for the publication of this book, it is my friend Dr. Abdul Ghafur. Apart from having been a long suffering listener to most of these speeches (and abetted a good few of them) year after year, it was he who suggested that they might be re-published in book form. He thought that these speeches were as innocent an exposition of archaeology and art as could be risked and might, therefore, be placed in the hands of the general reader without danger.

I was certainly not averse to publication; no author ever is. To start with, I had certain doubts, but these were soon subdued. It seemed to me that Dr. Ghafur had a point. The professional archaeologist, overburdened with knowledge and wisdom as he always is, has a tendency to get lost in the erudite technicalities of his subject, while a lay-man, blessed with a little learning and a great deal of ignorance, may say what he likes without doing much damage. The same is true of the professional art critic, who can always manage to say things without letting other people understand—an accomplishment not open to ordinary mortals.

What was even more convincing was Dr. Ghafur's argument that the speeches having been inflicted on the public once, the performance could be repeated with impunity.

The speeches on Archaeology were delivered at the annual sessions of the Museums Association of Pakistan, and most of those on art and literature at the annual meetings of the Pakistan Writers' Guild. Not being a member of the Guild I have been wondering why that august body should invite an outsider year after year, for the sole purpose of being harangued by him. The more I think about it, the more I am inclined to ascribe it to their good nature.

I have to express my gratitude to Professor Tucci who has found time to read the book and honour it with an introduction, in spite of the many preoccupations that take him more or less round the globe every year. If this book has any merit, it comes from the kind and encouraging words he has said about it. It is difficult to live up to his good opinion; one can only try.

Dr. Abdul Ghafur and Mr. B. A. Dar have, besides reading the proofs, re-checked references and helped in a number of other ways. They have taken a great deal of trouble and I am grateful to them.

Lastly, there is my friend Geoffrey Glaister. It is not only that he has made valuable suggestions; it is usual for friends to make them. (Like the true Englishman that he is, Mr. Glaister is as reticent with his suggestions as he is irresistible with them). Having read the proofs a number of times already, he also offered to do the final reading—an offer which, in a parasitic moment, I accepted. It certainly relieved me of the necessity of reading them myself! On top of everything, he gave the book its title and insisted on preparing the Index that appears at the end of the book. I do not think I could thank him adequately even if I were to try.

KARACHI,   **Mumtaz Hasan**
6th August, 1967

ILLUSTRATIONS

...sly described as 'noble man', 'high priest' and 'king', this steatite bust was recovered from Moenjodaro. (2500 B.C.-National Museum Karachi).

Mother Goddess. Terracotta. Moenjodaro, 2500-1800 B. C. (National Museum, Karachi).

A Seal from Moenjodaro. 2500 B. C. (Moenjodaro Site Museum).

Siddhartha fasting. This piece of Gandhara sculpture is renowned for its superb and forceful realism expressed in the face and body—4... century A. D. (Lahore Museum).

IN QUEST OF DAIBUL

Speech at the foundation stone—laying ceremony of the Site Museum at Bhambore
21 August, 1960

Lake and Citadel

It is a rare privilege for me to be here today. It was ten years ago, in December 1950, that I first visited Bhambore. The visit was inspired by a lecture which my friend, Dr. Nabi Bakhsh Baloch of the Sind University, delivered in Frere Hall, Karachi, under the chairmanship of the late Dr. Daudpota. In that lecture, Dr. Baloch traced the history of the quest for Daibul, the old port town of Sind which the Arab general, Muhammad bin Qasim, besieged and conquered in 711 A.D. Dr. Baloch referred to the various sites which scholars had investigated in the course of their enquiry. These sites included that of Bhambore[1] which had been referred to by General Cunningham in his *Ancient Geography* and had, among others, been examined by Cousens, the then Superintendent of the Western Archaeological Circle. Cousens thought that Bhambore was too small a place to have been the site of the flourishing city of Daibul, and that was the end of the site as far as he was concerned. Dr. Baloch, on the other hand, gave a number of reasons why Bhambore was a likely site for Daibul, although the reasons were based on philological argument rather than empirical evidence. Dr. Baloch thought, for example, that Bhambore was probably a corruption of Van-Vihar which signifies a Buddhist temple. Again, it is possible, Dr. Baloch felt, that the Arabic word *Khaur*, which stands for a gulf or a creek, might have been metamorphosed into Gharo, the sea creek near Bhambore. It may be relevant to recall that Ibn al-Athir, and other Arab historians, speak of the *Khaur-ad-Daibul* or Daibul creek. The location of the Gharo creek so close to Bhambore would thus lend significance to the speculation—and it is no more than speculation—that Bhambore and Daibul may be one and the same.

---

1. Also spelt as Banbhore

3

Inscribed handled cup
white paste pottery from Bhambore

Bluish green jar from
Bhambore 9th-11th century A.D. (National Museum)

I had the feeling, after listening to Dr. Baloch, that there was a *prima facie* case for starting excavations at Bhambore. Before making a move in the matter, however, I thought I must visit the site personally to see whether it was really as small and insignificant as Cousens had made it out to be. I wanted to come here anyway, for even if there was no archaeology in the place, there was no doubt about its having been the home of Sassi, the tragic heroine of the Sassi-Punnoo romance. Be that as it may, I came here for the first time on the 10th December 1950, in the company of a number of distinguished scholars, including the late Dr. Muhammad Nazim, and the late Qazi Ahmad Mian Akhtar. They both departed this life five years ago. How happy would they, and all of us, have been if they were alive today to see these wonderful excavations that lie around us.

None of us who saw these mounds on that December morning ten years ago had any hesitation in saying that the site was not at all small. Indeed, it was as big as any archaeologist could handle. A wag risked the uncharitable guess that Cousens, distinguished scholar and archaeologist that he was, had been punishing the bottle before he undertook to pass judgement on Bhambore!

Two days later, on the 12th of December, I wrote to the Ministry of Education suggesting excavations at Bhambore. That letter is still waiting for a reply, and if the Archaeological Department had not already provided the answer we have around us, I should have thought it was time to issue a reminder. As it happened, the Department took steps shortly afterwards to protect the site and investigations were conducted briefly by Alcock in 1951. Even before Alcock started his work, someone put out an enthusiastic story in the newspapers that Daibul had been discovered in Bhambore already, because pieces of Arab pottery and glass and some coins with Kufic-looking characters on them had been picked up from the site. This, to say the least, was a premature attempt at celebrating a possible discovery, a discovery which, incidentally, still rests in the lap of the future. It is a pity Alcock's explorations were not pursued further at the time although Muhammad Nazim wrote a report on them. This was the second time that the Bhambore excavations had been started and given up. The first time it happened was in 1928, when Majumdar, that ill-starred scholar who lost his life in the wilds of Sind, had his trial pits and trenches in Bhambore.

Since 1951, I had been hoping that the beginning made by Majumdar and Alcock, which touched the bare fringe of the site, would be carried further and full scale excavations of Bhambore would be undertaken. I said "hoping" because I had no authority over the Ministry of Education and could only hope. I did, of course, possess a certain power of persuasion which all Finance Ministry officials have when they speak to officials of other Ministries, but archaeologists (may their tribe increase!) are not ordinary mortals like you and me, and what may appear good argument to us may not appeal to them at all. To cut a long story short, it took me a good few years of talking and hoping before I succeeded in getting the right answer from the Department. Raoul Curiel, that eminent and lovable scholar whose friendship I am proud to claim, was then the Director of Archaeology, and it was on a fateful day, in the summer of 1957, that his heart melted. In that charming manner which is all his own, he told me that Bhambore was going to be excavated during the course of that budget year. He added, as an explanation, that there was only one man to whom he could entrust the task, and that was a gentleman by the name of Fazal Ahmad Khan. This Fazal Ahmad Khan had so far been busy doing miracles in Mainamati, Kot Diji and elsewhere and it had not therefore been possible for him earlier to bestow his attention on Bhambore.

It was in March, 1958, that the great day came when excavations started at Bhambore in right earnest, and the Department of

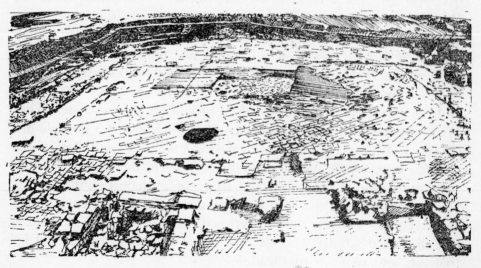

The Grand Mosque

6

Archaeology, having magnanimously forgiven my past importunities, asked me to inaugurate them. Since then, Bhambore has become a place of excitement. The excavations, which to start with, brought out a variety of Omayyad and Abbasid objects, including coins, pottery and glass, soon unearthed pre-Islamic and pre-Christian layers of occupation. Judging from some of the inscriptions we have discovered, it is probable that Bhambore possesses the oldest mosque of the Sub-continent. The first coin we found in Bhambore was a gold dinar of Wathiq Billah, (not the *Vathek* of Beckford's novel), coined in the year 229 A.H. (843-844 A.D.) Subsequently a number of silver and copper coins, including those of Hisham bin Abdul Malik and Al-Mamun, were discovered. It is clear from the progress of the excavations that the most glorious period of the Bhambore settlement is the Muslim period, the Hindu, Buddhist and other periods being comparatively poor. On the whole, the diggings have yielded a wealth of material already. Those of you who have had an opportunity of seeing the tented museum by yonder lake will be able to form some idea of the valuable objects that have been collected so far. This, I should surmise, is but an earnest of the great things that are still to come.

And now we shall have this Museum, of which the first stone is being laid today. It will be the custodian of the treasures of Bhambore, and I can already picture to myself the enthusiasm with which, before long, scholars and savants will come from far and near to see this house of wonders.

May I also hope that along with the Museum there will be a restaurant and a rest house. And a lake full of water, with a boat club to match. And last, though by no means least, a properly metalled road. Only if all these hopes and wishes are fulfilled will Bhambore come into its own.

And what about Daibul? You have already heard of the objects of the Omayyad and Abbasid periods, the coins of Hisham bin Abdul Malik and Wathiq Billah, the early Islamic pottery and above all, the ancient mosque and the numerous stone inscriptions which are waiting to be deciphered. It is also beyond doubt that this is a place with a history reaching back to the Hindu period, and with Scythian and Parthian associations. Nevertheless we are not yet in a position to say how near or how far we are from the discovery of Daibul, nor will the failure to find Daibul at Bhambore matter very much now.

7

Columbus was trying to find his way to India when he discovered America, and even if we do not discover Daibul at Bhambore, we have discovered Bhambore in any case. It may be some time before the exact identity of this place is established. It may turn out to be Pattala, that harbour where Alexander split his forces for the homeward journey, and it may turn out to be Daibul after all.* The discovery cannot elude us indefinitely. And if Daibul is not here, it must be somewhere not very far away. Eliot and Elphinstone thought it was at Karachi; Ferishta, Abul Fazal, Burton and Cousens thought it was at Thatta; Raverty thought it was at Pir Patho; Haig thought it was at Kakar Bukera, and others have thought of Mirpur Sakro, and other places. The Daibul hunt will continue. I wish we knew a little more fully than we do the Arab geographers' reckoning of longitudes and latitudes. That would help the enquiry. For it is not only Daibul that we are after; we have also to unearth the remains of other Arab settlements in Sind, such as Mahfuzah and Baiza. Where are these places? And where is Kiraj, the place where, as Baladhuri tells us, Muhammad bin Qasim's image was worshipped after his recall to Damascus? That is a strange example in history of a conquered people deifying and worshipping their conqueror, particularly when he was no longer in power. We know too little about the period of Arab civilisation in this Sub-continent which, in more than one respect, was the most remarkable phase of Muslim rule in this part of the world. Whatever little we know so far we owe to the pioneering work of that great scholar, Sulaiman Nadvi, whose researches have struck new paths in historical scholarship. European scholars have generally been attracted to Hindu and Buddhist archaeology and have not attached importance to the Muslim period. But we in Pakistan, while sharing European enthusiasm for the Hindu, Buddhist and other periods, are vitally concerned with Muslim archaeology and have to fill the gaps left by European scholars. We are particularly interested in the Arab dominion in Sind, and the Bhambore excavations are the first step in this direction. We now look to the archaeologists of Pakistan not only to help us, and the rest of the world, to know more about that great and glorious period of Muslim history, but also to develop a proper school of Muslim Archaeology in this Sub-continent.

---

*Since this was written, fourteen inscriptions have been studied and published by Dr. M. A. Ghafur who identifies Bhambore with Daibul. See "14 Kufic Inscriptions of Bhambore, the Site of Daibul," *Pakistan Archaeology*, No. 3, 1966.

An interior view of the Emperor Jehangir's tomb at Lahòre, completed in about 1637 by his son the Emperor Shahjehan, showing fresco decorations on walls and tessellated marble flooring.

Nur Jahan, the favourite and famous queen of Jahangir. (Mughul School 18th century A. D. - Lahore Museum)

MUSLIMS AND ARCHAEOLOGY

Presidential Address to the 15th Annual General Conference of the Museums Association of Pakistan at Hyderabad, March 1965

The Muslim love of history is derived from the Quran which repeatedly draws attention to the significance of historical events. It points again and again to the rise and fall of peoples as a phenomenon to be studied for guidance. It asks us to go forth into the world and see for ourselves the fate of those who were once powerful and proud, who rebelled against the Almighty and were destroyed for their wickedness. Yaqut Hamavi has told us how his whole life's inspiration came from a single verse of the Quran :

قل سيروا في الارض ثم انظروا كيف كان عاقبة المكذبين

Say : Travel through the earth
And see what was the end
Of those who rejected Truth.[1]

It was this verse which filled Yaqut with the desire to know as much of the world as he could and helped him to become one of the greatest geographers of all time.

The Quran repeatedly refers to the remains of ancient civilizations which have been preserved in the world, that we may learn to live in righteousness and humility :

وكم اهلكنا من قرية بطرت معيشتها فتلك مساكنهم لم تسكن من بعدهم الا قليلا

And how many populations
We destroyed, which exulted
In their life (of ease and plenty)!
Now those habitations of theirs,
After them, are deserted,
All but (miserable) few![2]

اولم يسيروا في الارض فينظروا كيف كان عاقبة الذين كانوا من قبلهم كانوا اشد منهم قوة
وآثاراً في الارض فاخذهم الله بذنوبهم وما كان لهم من الله من واق

Do they not travel
Through the earth and see
What was the End
Of those before them ?

1   *Holy Quran*, English translation by Yusuf Ali, Vol. I, VI. 11, Lahore, p. 291.
2   *Holy Quran*, ibid., Vol. II, XXVIII. 58, p. 1018.

They were even superior
To them in strength,
And in the traces (they
Have left) in the land.
But God did call them
To account for their sins,
And none had they
To defend them against God. [3]

In the Chapter entitled *Yunus*, the dying Pharaoh is told that his body will be preserved by God as an example to posterity :

وجاوزنا ببنى اسرائيل البحر فاتبعهم فرعون وجنوده بغياً وعدواً حتى اذا ادركه الغرق قال
آمنت انه لا اله الا الذى آمنت به بنو اسرائيل وانا من المسلمين الئن وقد عصيت من قبل وكنت
من المفسدين ۰ فاليوم ننجيك ببدنك لتكون لمن خلفك آية وان كثيرا من الناس عن آياتنا لغفلون

We took the Children
Of Israel across the sea ;
Pharaoh and his hosts followed them
In insolence and spite.
At length, when overwhelmed
With the flood, he said :
"I believe that there is no god
Except Him Whom the Children
Of Israel believe in :
I am of those who submit
(To God in Islam)".
"Ah now !—But a little while
Before, wast thou in rebellion !
And thou didst mischief (and violence) !
This day shall We save thee
In thy body, that thou
Mayest be a sign to those
Who come after thee !
But verily, many among mankind
Are heedless of our Signs ! [4]

Similarly, in the Traditions of the Prophet, we find that when he

---

3 *Holy Quran*, ibid., Vol. III, XL. 21, p. 1268.
4 *Holy Quran*, ibid., Vol. II, X. 90-92, p. 507.

passed near Hijr he asked his companions not to stop there as the people of that place had been punished by the Almighty for their sins :

عن ابن عمر لما مر النبى بالحجر قال لا تدخلوا مساكن الذين ظلموا انفسهم ان يصيبكم ما اصابهم الا ان تكونوا باكين · ثم تقنّع راسه واسرع السير حتى جاز الوادى

"It is related by Ibn Umar that when the Prophet, on whom be peace, passed Hijr, he said to his companions, 'do not enter the houses of those who had committed inquity, lest you suffer their fate, except that you may enter weeping'. Saying this, he covered his face and passed quickly through the valley." [5]

As a result of the moral emphasis placed by the Quran on past events and the visible remains of ancient civilizations, historical and archaeological research has become an inherent part of the tradition of Muslim culture. Muslim historians and geographers in their accounts of various periods and places have left us detailed records of great archaeological importance ; indeed, we owe to them the greater part of our knowledge of the Afro-Asian world in ancient and mediaeval times.

There is a wealth of archaeological knowledge in the works of historians like Yaqubi, Al-Tabari, Baladhuri and Ibn al-Athir, and geographers like Istakhri, Maqdisi, Masudi and Yaqut. Le Strange [6] has given us a detailed picture of the historical geography of Mesopotamia, Iran and Central Asia, as it emerges from the work of Muslim geographers and historians. The work of Ibn Khaldun, the world's first and probably greatest philosophical historian and the father of modern sociology, contains a scientific account of the evolution of the social and religious institutions of mankind. Geographers like Ibn Khurdadbih and Ibn Rustah have recorded for our benefit detailed descriptions of ancient road systems, which help us to identify lost trade routes and vanished centres of civilization. One of the notable contributions made by Muslim scholars is the study of individual cities in their historical, geographical and archaeological aspects. Ibn Asakir's history of Damascus and Khatib's history of Baghdad are not the only examples of their kind. We have much earlier works

---

5 Sahih Bukhari, *Kitab-ul-Maghazi*, Cairo Edition.
6 Le Strange, *Lands of the Eastern Caliphate* and *Baghdad Under the Abbasids*.

13

like Azraqi's *Akhbar-u-Makka* [7] which can compare with the best archaeological guide books of today on Athens, Rome or Paris. Further research may establish Azraqi as the pioneer in this particular field. One of his interesting observations relates to the crown and throne of "Kabul Shah" or the king of Kabul, which had been placed on display in the Kaaba by order of Al-Mamum, with inscriptions narrating the glorious victory of Islam, which Azraqi has copied for us in his book. The inscriptions are of great importance for the history of the Arab conquest of Kabul and the north western frontier of this Sub-continent. Al Maqrizi's *Kitab-ul-Khitat* [8] gives a detailed account of towns and villages, roads and streets and important monuments of ancient Egypt.

There are innumerable works dealing with other cities, their important tombs, mosques and monuments. The accounts of Muslim travellers are another important source of historical and archaeological information. Ibn Battuta, who kept globe-trotting for thirty years and covered more distance than any other human being before the age of steam, has given us a detailed and dependable picture of the India of Muhammad bin Tughlaq. This great traveller had a feeling for ancient monuments and inscriptions. While passing through Bukhara he copied a number of inscriptions from the ancient graveyard of the city, although unluckily he lost them in his later travels. He also copied the inscription of the Masjid Quwwat-ul-Islam of Delhi.[9] Even the saints and mystics of Islam have not been without interest in archaeology. A well known example is that of Dhu-un-Nun Misri, who, according to Jami, represents a turning point in the history of Sufism, and who had a scholarly interest in old Egyptian temples and their inscriptions.[10]

Muslim rulers, besides being great builders themselves, have always taken deep interest in ancient monuments. We find, for instance, that when Al-Mamun, the Abbasid Caliph, entered Egypt and saw the Pyramids, he had the great Pyramid of Cheops opened to know what was within.[11] This was not the first attempt of its kind.

---

7   *Akhbar-u-Makka*, by Abil Walid Muhammad Bin Abdullah bin Ahmad-ul-Azraqi, edited by Rushdi Saleh and published by Al Matba Majidiya in 1352 H.

8   *Kitab-ul-Khitat*, Maktaba Ihayaul Uloom, Lebanon.

9   Ibn Battuta. *The Rehla* translated by Mahdi Husain, Baroda 1953, pp. 50-80.

10   Abdur Rahman Jami, *Nafahat-ul-Uns*.

11   John Greaves, *The World of the Past*, Vol. I, p. 521. Also Al Maqrizi's *Kitab-ul-Khitat*, Vol. I, p. 201.

Before Mamun, Abdul Aziz bin Marwan, brother of the Omayyad Caliph Abdul Malik and Governor of Egypt, had gone to some trouble to investigate the treasures of the Pyramids. Although his investigations were not as scientific or fruitful as the work of the archaeologists of our own time, Abdul Aziz bin Marwan may be regarded as the man who led the way to Egyptology. It has to be remembered that his attack on the mysteries of the Pyramids occurred more than a thousand years before Napoleon's invasion of Egypt, which marks the first awakening of serious interest on the part of Europe in them. Maqrizi tells us of some of the wonders that were discovered by Abdul Aziz. Subsequently, a number of local potentates, including Muhammad bin Tafaj of the Akhsheed dynasty and the famous Ahmad bin Tulun, devoted considerable attention to these great Egyptian monuments.[12]

These archaeological investigations were inspired by scientific curiosity as well as by the quest for buried treasure. It is only fair to add that the prospect of unearthing underground wealth has lured the antiquarian through the ages, and notwithstanding the more scientific attitude that has developed in the twentieth century, it continues to influence archaeological research down to this day. Indeed, it may be true to say that archaeology as a science has developed out of the treasure-hunting impulse.

It has been the favourite hobby of Muslim rulers all over the world to build new monuments :

ہر کہ آمدہ عمارتِ نو ساخت

Whoever comes builds anew.

We have had builders like Harun al-Rashid the Abbasid, Abdur Rahman the Third of Spain, and Shah Jahan the Magnificent, the like of whom the world has seldom seen.

At the same time, there has been a tradition of respect for ancient tombs, mosques and other monuments. It is true that there have been regrettable departures from that tradition on more than one occasion, and we have had such outbreaks of savagery as the wholesale desecration of Omayyad tombs by the Abbasids. For-

---

12 Maqrizi, ibid. pp 71-73. Although the author does not mention the word 'Pyramid' in the text, his description leaves little doubt that it was one of the pyramids.

tunately for us, such instances are few and far between, and have not met with approval. The importance attached by the Muslims generally to ancient relics and monuments is reflected in the work of a number of poets belonging to various periods. An Arab poet says :

تلك آثارنا تدلّ علينا   فانظر واعد ناللي الاثار

These are our works, these works our souls display.
Behold our work when we have passed away.

Khaqani composed a *qasidah* on the ruins of Ctesiphon, the capital of the Sassanids, which begins : [13]

هان ای دل عبرت بین، از دیده نظر کن هان   ایوان مدائن را آئینه عبرت دان

Behold and take example, O heart, look close,
Behold the palaces of Madain, and take a lesson.

Urfi says :

از نقش و نگار در و دیوار شکسته   آثار پدید است صناديع عجم را

The decorations on ancient ruins
Tell us of the lost glory of the great ones of Ajam.

These are only a few examples. The general Muslim attitude towards old relics and monuments is expressed in Saadi's famous verse :[14]

نام نیک رفتگان ضائع مکن   تا بماند نام نیکت برقرار

Let not the good name of those that are gone fall into oblivion.
'Tis thus that thy own good name shall endure.

In the Indo-Pakistan Sub-continent, historiography, in the proper sense, begins with the advent of Islam. In the beginning of the eighth century A.D., with the Arab occupation of Sind, we come into contact for the first time with the scientific and historical traditions of Muslim culture. The detailed observations of the Muslim geographers and historians of this Sub-continent, like Sulaiman Tajir, Abu Zaid Hasan Sirafi, Masudi, Istakhri, Maqdisi, Baladhuri and Alberuni, in regard to pre-Islamic cultures and civilizations in this

---

13 *Kuliyat Khaqani*, ed. by Ali Abdul Rasuli, Teheran Edition, p. 362.
14 *Kuliyat Saadi*, edited by Muhammad Ali Farughi, Teheran 1340.

16

part of the world, based as they are on personal experience, can help the student of history even today to reconstruct, with fair accuracy, the social and religious institutions of those times. The description of monuments like the temple of Daibul that we find in Baladhuri, is an extremely valuable guide for archaeological research today. Abu Raihan Albiruni, a protege of Mahmud of Ghazna, took up the study of Sanskrit as a discipline for scholarly research into the various sects of the Hindus, their beliefs, their habits and culture patterns, and has left us, in his *Kitab al-Hind*, a primary source of historical material for the study of pre-Islamic India. This is a service to the cause of human knowledge, which entitles Alberuni to be regarded as the first Indologist of the world.

Even though, with the end of the Arab occupation, the cultural tradition underwent a change in certain respects, the study of history and archaeology continued to make progress under the Turks, Afghans and Mughals, who succeeded the Arabs. The most outstanding builder and preserver of monuments in the early period of Muslim rule in the Sub-continent was Firoz Shah Tughlaq, who had repairs carried out to the old tombs and mausoleums of a number of kings and saints. This may partly have been due to religious considerations, but it certainly served the cause of archaeology. One of his remarkable acts was the removal of two Asoka pillars from their original sites to Delhi, where they are preserved to this day.[15] The propriety of removing the pillars from their original locations is open to question, but although we may feel that it would have been better to protect and preserve them where they were, it is hardly fair to apply the ideas of the twentieth century to the fourteenth. In any case, posterity owes a debt of gratitude to Firoz Shah for having preserved these pillars.

It is difficult, within the short space of time available, to speak of all the Muslim rulers who showed active interest in the preservation of ancient monuments. It may, however, not be out of place to mention Aurangzeb, a number of whose *farmans* are in existence, giving grants for the maintenance of old temples, at the same time as they prohibited the construction of new ones. His famous Benares *farman* of 1069 A.H. is particularly relevant.[16] Tippu Sultan was

---

15 S. Moinul Haq, *A Short History of the Sultanate of Delhi*, Karachi 1956, pp. 148-49.
16 S.M. Jafar "Religious Views of Akbar and Aurangzeb," in *Proceedings of the All-Pakistan History Conference*, 1957, p. 271.

another Muslim ruler who took care to preserve Hindu temples and gave grants to a number of them.[17]

When after ruling in the Sub-continent for twelve centuries, the Muslims were subdued by the British, they lost all they had, their educational system, their cultural tradition, their lands, their properties. They were no longer in a position to look after the monuments they had built, and in their helplessness, began to feel some concern for the magnificent relics of their imperial past. Syed Ahmad Khan, that great leader who is the first architect of Pakistan, was also the first to give his attention to the ancient monuments of Muslim times, which, for want of proper maintenance, were crumbling and falling away. He made a detailed study of the old buildings and monuments in Delhi and took considerable pains to record measurements and inscriptions. Imam Buksh Sahbaee, the well-known Persian scholar and poet, tells us how the Syed used to hoist himself with the help of long poles to the level of the Qutub Minar inscriptions, a position which was so precarious as to keep Sahbaee praying for the Syed's safety.[18] The result of these labours was the *Athar al-Sanadid*, a book which contains the first systematic account of the monuments of Delhi. With the completion of this work Syed Ahmad Khan became the father of Muslim archaeology in this Sub-continent.

Qutub Minar Delhi

British interest in India's past goes back to the days of the East India Company. Men like Sir William Jones ('Asiatic Jones' as he is called), the great founder of the Asiatic Society of Bengal, who was incidentally a Chief Justice; James Prinsep, the Calcutta Mint Master turned numismatician who started the *Journal* of the Asiatic Society, and other scholars reflected the growing enthusiasm of eighteenth century Europe for the study of past civilizations. There are other

17   S. Moinul Haq, (ed.) *Basair* (*Tippu Sultan Number*), Karachi, p. 195.
18   Ahmad Mian Akhtar Junagari, *Sir Sayyed Ka Ilmi Karnama*, published by Muslim Education Conference, Karachi.

Europeans besides the British such as General Ventura, the Italian soldier of fortune who flourished at the court of Ranjit Singh and who was the first to dig into Buddhist stupas even though for treasure. A proper and systematic organization for archaeological work was, however, not set up till 1862, when Major-General Sir Alexander Cunningham, a distinguished officer of the Royal Engineers, was appointed Director of Archaeology and required "to make an accurate description of such remains as most deserve notice, with the history of them so far as it is traceable and a record of the traditions that are retained regarding them." In 1874, he was designated Director-General of the Archaeological Survey of India and his functions were enlarged. He was now "to superintend a complete search over the whole country and a systematic record and description of all architectural and other remains that are remarkable alike for their antiquity or their beauty, or their historic interest."

His jurisdiction, however, was confined to Northern India till 1874, when it was nominally extended over the rest of the country, with Dr. Burgess holding charge of Bombay and Madras Presidencies under him. General Cunningham, whose interest lay predominantly in Buddhist archaeology, performed his task with great ability and success, even though he lacked the help of proper staff. He produced as many as 23 volumes of reports descriptive of 23 years of his archaeological tours in Central and Northern India.[19] "As Mariette was the father and founder of archaeology in Egypt," says Abu Imam, "so was Cunningham of the Indian Archaeological Survey. As Schliemann followed Pausanias, so did Cunningham follow Hsuan Tsang and Fa-Hsien. Like Rawlinson and Morris, he was a great decipherer of scripts. Like Raoul Rochtette he was a great numismatist."[20]

In 1881, under a scheme initiated by Lord Lytton, another post was created with the designation of 'Curator of Ancient Monuments' and Major A.H. Cole was appointed to it. Between the years 1881-84, he produced three reports formulating a valuable programme of conservation work for the future. He was also responsible for 22 yearly preliminary reports on monuments in the Bombay and Madras Presi-

19 Sir John Cumming (ed.), *Revealing India's Past*, London 1939, pp. 1-13.
20 Abu Imam, "Sir Alexander Cunningham (1814-1893): The first phase of Indian Archaeology," *J. R. A. S.*, London, 1963, pp. 194-206.

dencies, Rajputana, Hyderabad and the Punjab and for ten folio volumes which appeared under the title *Preservation of National Monuments in India* (1881-85). As early as 1883 we hear of a Muslim excavator, Jomadar Kaleh Khan, who quite independently conducted excavations in Mardan district. In the words of Major Cole, "Kaleh Khan has had great experience in excavation of Buddhist stupas and monasteries both in Yousufzai and in the Khyber and has a remarkably keen nose for a find."[21] After General Cunningham's retirement in 1885, Dr. Burgess became Director-General. Although he carried out comparatively few excavations his method of study in architecture and epigraphy was sound. His reports were much better produced and much more systematic than those of Cunningham. He was the first archaeologist in this Sub-continent to make extensive use of the recently developed art of photography in his reporting. He had vision and imagination enough to have been instrumental in starting the two well-known journals—*The Indian Antiquary* and *The Epigraphica Indica*. During his tenure of office, Dr. E. Huetsch was appointed Epigraphist for the translation of inscriptions in the Sanskrit, Pali and Dravidian languages.

In 1889, Dr. Burgess retired. Although he had rendered valuable services in various capacities for 15 years, the Department of Archaeology was yet to be organized properly. Indeed, by the time Dr. Burgess retired, the Department had already fallen a victim to the retrenchment policies of the Finance Department and placed on a care and maintenance basis. In 1895, the Government of India had second thoughts in regard to the future of the Department and decided upon a fresh re-organization. The whole of the country was divided into five Survey Circles, namely, Madras, Bombay with Sind and Berar, the Punjab with Baluchistan and Ajmer, the United Provinces with the Central Provinces and Bengal with Assam. The scheme came into force in May 1899. But even before that date, the newly appointed Viceroy, Lord Curzon, had, in the words of Sir John Marshall, made it clear that a new era was dawning for Indian archaeology and that his government would not long be content with the half-measures envisaged in the scheme. Lord Curzon, who is easily the greatest patron of archaeology during the whole course of British rule in this Sub-continent, regarded the preservation and maintenance of ancient monuments as an imperial

---

21 H.H. Cole, *Memorandum on Ancient Monuments in Eusofzai*, Simla, Government Press, 1883. p. 9

responsibility in the highest sense. He took conservation of monuments away from the Public Works Department of the Provinces and entrusted it to the Central Government. He attached almost equal importance to the exploration and study of all classes of ancient remains, to the excavation of buried sites, to the copying and reading of inscriptions and to the provision and adequate equipment of museums. "Epigraphy," he said in a memorable speech, "should not be set behind research any more than research should be set behind conservation. All are ordered parts of any scientific scheme of antiquarian work. I am not one of those who think that Government can afford to patronize the one and ignore the other. It is, in my judgement, equally our duty to dig and discover, to classify, reproduce and describe, to copy and decipher and to cherish and conserve." The Viceroy set about his task by securing greater resources of men and money for the newly organized Archaeological Department.[22] The most important step he took in this direction was the appointment of Mr. J. H. (afterwards Sir John) Marshall.

A brilliant classical scholar from Cambridge, John Marshall had been associated with excavations in Crete and was preparing for further explorations in Asia Minor, when Lord Curzon offered him the post of Director-General of Archaeology in India. He was no more than twenty five at the time. For the next thirty years, he headed the Archaeological Department with rare distinction and to the lasting benefit of archaeology in this Sub-continent. He carried

Sir John Marshall

through systematic and far-reaching schemes for the conservation of a large number of famous buildings, including the groups of Muslim palaces, mosques and tombs at Delhi, Agra, Lahore and Ajmer, the well-known capital of the Kings of Malva at Mandu, the Buddhist stupas at Sanchi, the groups of Hindu temples at Khajuraho in India and the palace of Mandalay in Burma. He restored and re-designed the ancient gardens attached to many of the Mughal tombs. His most important achievement is undoubtedly his spectacular discovery of the Indus Valley Civilization at Mohenjo-daro[23] and Harappa and

22 Sir John Cumming (ed.), op. cit., p. 30
23 This place name is also spelled as Moenjo-daro.

21

Taxila—view of the great stupa from north west

A view of the excavation at Harappa

the successive civilizations of the Persians, Scythians, Parthians and Kushans at Taxila. Apart from his work in the field of conservation and excavation, Sir John Marshall was responsible for introducing a scheme of archaeological scholars to provide training and opportunity for talented young men of the country. This scheme was prepared in accordance with the general policy of Lord Curzon who, with rare foresight, had come to realise that the British regime in India was not destined to last for more than a few decades.[24] It is to this training scheme that we owe such distinguished Muslim scholars

24 Sir John Marshall, "The Story of the Archaeological Department of India" in Sir John Cumming (Ed.), op. cit.pp. 1-33.

22

as the late Syed Ghulam Yazdani, the eminent epigraphist of Muslim inscriptions in the Sub-continent and editor of the *Epigraphica Indomoslemica* from 1915 to 1941, whose work on pre-Muslim India, particularly Ajanta and Ellora, is no less important than his researches on the Muslim period.[25] Another distinguished scholar produced by the scheme was the late Khan Bahadur Zafar Hasan, whose work on the Delhi monuments, on Muslim coins and Muslim calligraphy is of abiding value.

In the time of Marshall a number of European scholars distinguished themselves in various fields. Henry Cousens has important contributions to his credit in the field of Hindu and Muslim archaeology. He published a number of important works, of which *The Antiquities of Sind*, which pertains exclusively to Pakistan, deserves particular mention. The name of Sir Aurel Stein (1862-1948) stands high in the history of archaeological exploration of Baluchistan and the north west frontier of Pakistan. His monumental work includes *Innermost Asia, On Alexander's Track to the Indus, Old Routes to Western Iran, Ser India, Archaeological Tour in Waziristan, Archaeological Tour in Gedrosia* which still serve as a beacon light to the archaeological explorer of today. Dr. J.Ph. Vogel, the Superintendent of the Northern

A mosaic tile from Lahore Fort

Circle, was the first archaeologist to recommend to the then Government of India, on the 20th of June, 1910, protection of the world famous site of Taxila. His excavations at Charsadda in 1902 and his scholarly work *Tile Mosaics of Lahore Fort* are substantial contributions to the archaeology of Pakistan. He served as honorary assistant to the Lahore Museum and arranged its Graeco-Buddhist gallery. A. Foucher is one of the pioneer scholars who pursued researches on Gandhara Art. His *Graeco-BuddhistArt of Gandhara* is an outstanding contribution to the ancient history of Pakistan and we are similarly indebted to Konor for his *Kharoshthi Inscriptions.*

We in Pakistan have particular reason to be grateful to Sir John Marshall as the main archaeological sites we inherited on indepen-

---

25 Ahmad Hasan Dani, *Ancient Pakistan*, Vol. I, Peshawar, 1964.

dence, namely Mohenjo-daro, Harappa and Taxila in West Pakistan and Paharpur and Mahasthangarh in East Pakistan, were excavated during his regime. Of these, he conducted the excavations at Taxila and Mohenjo-daro himself. His voluminous reports on Taxila and Mohenjo-daro are classics of scientific description and analysis. Before his death in 1958, he was able to complete his *Buddhist Art of Gandhara* and to revise, at the request of our Archaeological Department, his famous *Guide to Taxila*. The memorial plaque placed by the Pakistan Government for Sir John Marshall in the Taxila Museum is only a small token of this country's appreciation of the work of this great scholar. It is to be hoped that this will be followed by a fuller recognition of his contribution to Pakistan's archaeology.

Sir John Marshall retired from India in 1932 and was followed by Mr. Hargreaves, Rai Bahadur Daya Ram Sahni, Major Blakiston, Rao Bahadur K.N. Dikshit and Sir Mortimer Wheeler respectively. During the administration of these officers, the work of Sir John Marshall was carried forward and expanded. Among the new sites excavated, as far as the Pakistan areas are concerned, may be mentioned Khairpur and Bhambore. Sir Mortimer Wheeler, easily the most outstanding successor of Sir John Marshall, brought to bear on his task a new technique in excavation, known as the vertical technique, which has since been widely recognised and applied all over the world.

The Archaeological Department under Sir John Marshall was able to attract scholars of such distinction as Muhammad Nazim, the author of that classical work on Mahmud of Ghazna and editor of a number of *Memoirs* on Muslim Epigraphy, Mr. Hamid Qureshi, the author of valuable Memoirs on the Monuments of Bihar and of numerous papers on Hindu and Buddhist archaeology, and Maulvi Ashfaq Ali, the famous Curator of Delhi Fort and an authority on Mughal Painting. The archaeological explorations of R.D. Banerjee contributed towards the identification of the Indus Valley Civilization at Mohenjo-daro. The excavations conducted at Harappa by M.S. Vats and Daya Ram Sahni made a valuable contribution to the study of the Indus Valley Civilization. The systematic exploration of Sind by N.G. Majumdar, whose brilliant career was cut short by a premature and tragic death, deserves special mention. His work *Explorations in Sind* continues to be indispensible for the archaeological investigators of this region. The names of Dr. Ansari, archaeological

24

The Author with Professor Tucci

Monsieur Curiel (*left*) *the author*
(*centre*)*and* Dr. *F. A. Khan* (*right*)

engineer and author of valuable notes on the problems of conservation, and Khan Bahadur Sanaullah, the distinguished archaeological
chemist of the Sub-continent, are prominent in the field of Archaeological Science. The name of Mr. A.H. Khan, a distinguished architect of the Department, also deserves mention. Easily the most outstanding work in exploration and listing of sites and monuments was
that of Khan Bahadur Mian Wasiuddin in the Frontier Circle. On
the excavation side, mention may be made of Mr. Ghulam Qadir, and
Khan Sahib A.D. Siddiqi, the Excavation Assistant of Sir John
Marshall, whose services have received Sir John's appreciation in his
famous three volume report on Taxila. The Khan Sahib's memory
lives in the "S.D." Sector of Mohenjo-daro which has been named
after him.

The fourteenth of August, 1947, saw the emergence of Pakistan
as a sovereign independent state. The Government of the new
country had to face a number of problems, not the least among which
was lack of money.

The financial problem was accentuated by India's refusal to
give Pakistan its share of the cash balances of the undivided Government, and even when, after a great deal of public controversy,
Pakistan's claim was largely satisfied, the finances of the country were
none too easy. With its meagre resources Pakistan was called upon

25

to absorb the mass influx of Muslim population from across the border and, at the same time, to shoulder its defence responsibilities, which included not only the most strategic frontiers of undivided India, but also, unfortunately, the uneasy border with India itself. It is small wonder that when the Department of Archaeology came to be organized in Pakistan, it was no more than a skeleton affair, with Mr. Q.M. Muneer, a well-known scholar and epigraphist, as the first Director. He was followed in 1948 by Dr. Muhammad Nazim, who served for three months and gave place to Moulvi Shamsuddin Ahmad, the distinguished epigraphist and scholar, whose *Inscriptions of Bengal* and the catalogue of Muslim coins in the Indian Museum, Calcutta, are well known.

It was in Moulvi Shamsuddin's time that Sir Mortimer Wheeler was appointed as a part-time Adviser on Archaeology by the Pakistan Government and served as such for two years. His advice was as invaluable as his leadership. He guided the Department's activity within the limited resources available, and, under his direction, a beginning was made with the National Museum of Pakistan. He introduced Pakistan's archaeology to the world with his well known *Five Thousand Years of Pakistan*. In 1950, he made a pioneering attempt at deep digging at Mohenjo-daro.

Moulvi Shamsuddin was Director for five years, but his regime, like those of his predecessors, suffered from lack of men and money. He was succeeded in 1954 by Monsieur Raoul Curiel who had been specially recruited from France by the Pakistan Government. Monsieur Curiel, an outstanding archaeologist, the profundity of whose

Floral and geometrical carving in relief on Chawkandi Tombs

Tomb of Jan Baba, Makli, Thatta

Chawkandi tombs showing exquisite floral and geometrical carving in relief (17th, 18th century A.D.)

scholarship is matched only by his innate modesty, served Pakistan and the Department of Archaeology for four years as Director and, for a short while afterwards, as Archaeological Adviser. His regime was characterised by phenomenal progress on all sides. He organised the whole Department on a proper basis and gave life to the dead bones of archaeology. Conservation work, which badly needed attention, was placed on a systematic footing. The Chawkandi Tombs and a large part of the Makli graveyard was cleaned up and put into shape. In the Lahore Fort, under the knowledgeable and enthusiastic leadership of Mr. Waliullah Khan, the accretions of the Sikh and British periods were removed from a number of buildings in order to bring out the beauty of the original Mughal design. The Jindan Haveli has now been completely renovated as a part of the same operation to house the famous Princess Bamba Collection for which negotiations were started by Monsieur Curiel and which has since been acquired. This renovation in itself is a remarkable work of scientific conservation-cum-restoration. A number of lost masoncrafts like *Ghalib Kari* (stalactite work), brick-cut *Jali* work and glazed plaster work (*pukki Qalai*) were in consequence revived. Similarly, a beginning was made with repairs and renovations in the Shalimar Gardens and an illumination scheme sponsored both for the Gardens and the

Residence of Iqbal, McLeod Road, Lahore

Fort. This is now beginning to bear fruit, at least as far as the Shalimar is concerned. It was also decided to acquire the McLeod Road residence of Iqbal, where he produced his most important political and philosophical work, and where he wrote his address for the All-India Muslim League Session at Allahabad in 1930, in which he put forward the idea of Pakistan.

At the same time, important new excavations were undertaken at Mainamati, Kot Diji and Bhambore by Dr. F.A. Khan, then Superintendent of Exploration. The Museum Administration was reorganised and expanded. The National Museum of Pakistan which is now in the careful hands of Mr. S.A. Naqvi, the distinguished museologist of Pakistan, was built up through the efforts of a Committee appointed for the acquisition of antiquities, on which the Director himself functioned as Expert Member. The Committee operated on a Fund set apart for the purpose by the Central Government. Some of the acquisitions, such as the unique Abdul Malik coin, and the rare and unique manuscripts of the Zafar Hasan collection, were the result of Monsieur Curiel's personal efforts and direction. The rare manuscripts and coins of the Faizullah Collection were also acquired in his time. The National Museum, round which gathered a circle of friends and admirers of all races and religions, some of whom have done a great deal of volunteer work, soon entered the world class with its rare and unique though comparatively small collection. Among the ladies who have devoted their time and attention to the National Museum readily, honorarily and voluntarily, special mention should be made of Mrs. Rice and Mrs.

Bunting. A great friend of the Museum and the Department is Mr. Glaister of the British Council whose unfailing kindness and generous help on a number of occasions has been of inestimable value. Plans were made for site museums at a number of places, including Mohenjo-daro, Bhambore, Mainamati and Umarkot and construction was under-taken at some of the sites. Site museums were built or rebuilt at places like Mainamati and Mohenjo-daro. A small but comfortable Rest House was built at Makli. A fine library was built up in the Department, under Monsieur Curiel's loving care. With its anno-tated catalogue and cumulative periodical indexing it is rightly regar-ded, not only by its devoted librarian, Mirza Mahmud Baig, but also by the world at large, as the finest library on Art and Archaeology in the country. Through the generosity of Mr. Hoshang Dinshaw, the Dastur Dhalla Library, which represents the best collection on Zoroastrianism and Iranistics available in the country, now forms part of the Archaeological Library.

With Monsieur Curiel's influence, important links were forged with international organizations. A number of selected foreign archaeological missions were allowed to operate on various impor-tant sites to supplement the activities of the Department itself. The work of Professor Giuseppe Tucci and his Italian team in Swat, of Dr. Henry Field in Baluchistan and Bahawalpur, of Sir Mortimer Wheeler at Charsadda and of Monsieur Casal at Amri, is too well-known to need detailed description. A beginning was made with Pakistan's Archaeological Exhibitions abroad, which were sent to a number of countries. The services of an expert were obtained from UNESCO to help in studying the problems of conservation of monuments in Pakistan.

It was during Monsieur Curiel's time that Mr. Muhammad Idris Siddiqi, a distinguished officer of the Department, wrote the first book in Urdu on the Indus Valley Civilization. Mr. Muhammad Idris also produced a valuable *Guide to Thatta*. Sir John Marshall's revised edition of his *Guide to Taxila* also appeared during Monsieur Curiel's regime. These publications had the effect of promoting public interest in Pakistan's archaeology.

An outstanding event of the Curiel regime was the Exhibition of Islamic Art and Culture which was opened at the Lahore Fort by the President of Pakistan in December 1957 and which was subsequently held at Frere Hall, Karachi. To it came exhibits from Iran, Turkey, Indonesia, Great Britain, France, Italy, the United States and East and West Pakistan. It was a unique occasion and the variety of the objects exhibited and their rare and representative character made the Exhibition a memorable success.

Another important measure of the Curiel regime was the revival of the Archaeological Scholars' Scheme started by Sir John Marshall which had fallen into disuse in Pakistan. Young men, fresh from the University, were trained as probationers. They started on the humbler tasks of the Department to equip themselves for scientific investigation and discovery. Promising and able young officers of the department, like Dr. Abdul Ghafur and Dr. Nazimuddin, were sent for foreign studies and training.

During Monsieur Curiel's time, we often heard of a distinguished excavator, named Dr. F. A. Khan, whose work was evident at more than one site. It was this Dr. Khan, who succeeded Monsieur Curiel as Director of Archaeology in 1958. During the six years that have since elapsed, the Department has built further on the strong foundations laid by Monsieur Curiel and made remarkable progress under the new Director, whose reputation and achievement as an excavator have added new lustre to archaeology in the country.

An archaeological laboratory has been set up at Lahore. This has served to remedy one of the serious deficiencies of the Department on the scientific side. A team of young scholars has been trained abroad in archaeological chemistry, museology and anthropology. A number of archaeological exhibitions have been sent to foreign countries and have been a great success in Germany, Holland, Italy, the U.S.A., Ceylon and Japan. Scientific catalogues have been published for each of these exhibitions.

The Department has taken long strides in the development and scientific display of some ten museums including Swat, Harappa, Mohenjo-daro, Umarkot, Bhambore and two remarkable galleries in Jindan Haveli in the Lahore Fort in West Pakistan; and Mainamati, Mahasthangarh and Chittagong in East Pakistan. For all these, new buildings have been designed and constructed by the department itself. Rare objects have been acquired for the National and other Museums. Mr. Fazal Qadir has been prominent among the officers responsible for the display arrangements in site museums. Two site libraries have been established at Taxila and Swat and a third is contemplated at Mohenjo-daro. A library is also being set up at Iqbal's residence at McLeod Road, Lahore, which has now been acquired and renovated by the Department. In Chittagong, an Ethnographical Museum is being set up with a select library of its own. This museum will be greatly helped by the growing interest of scholars like Dr. Nazimuddin and Mr. A.B. Rajput in the primitive tribes of Pakistan. They are the first Pakistanis to turn to this subject. The work of epigraphy is developing under the scholarly leadership of Dr. Ghafur. Further excavations have been undertaken and more foreign archaeological missions provided facilities for work.

A number of new foreign archaeological missions have been allowed to work on various sites. The British, American and Japanese missions at Charsadda, Mohenjo-daro and the Makran coast and Mardan are particularly worth mention. The services of UNESCO experts have been obtained to help in tackling the problem of waterlogging and salinity at Mohenjo-daro. The work of publications, which had been initiated by Monsieur Curiel, has now been organized and concentrated in a new section in the office of the Director of Archaeology. *Pakistan Archaeology*, the new annual journal of the Department, gives an account of the Department's scientific work for the benefit of scholars in other parts of the world. Under the leadership of Dr. Khan, the Publications Branch of the Department has received a new impetus. He has himself made valuable contributions in various fields of archaeology. Apart from preliminary reports on excavations at Kot Diji, Bhambore and Mainamati, he has published *Fresh Side-lights on the Indus Valley Civilization*, and a number of articles on Pakistan's archaeology in international journals. The Department has also published a number of other studies, such as Waliullah's *Sikh Shrines*, Dani's *Sculptures from East Pakistan* and Patterson's *Soan, the Palaeolithic in Pakistan*.

Outside the Department, important works have been produced on History and Museology by, among others, a scholar of the eminence of Mr. S.M. Jafar. A welcome development is the increased interest in History and Archaeology in the Universities. The introduction of Archaeology as a Faculty in the Peshawar University is an important step in this direction. Dr. A.H. Dani, the well-known scholar in pre-history and an internationally recognised authority on Indology, is the Chairman and under his distinguished leadership, we can rightly expect great things.

A general view of the tomb of Shah Rukn-i-Alam, Multan. 1320-24 A.D. This highly ornate monument is representative of the Tughlaq period.

Queen Maya giving birth to Prince Siddaratha—(the original name of Buddha)—one of the most exquisite specimens of Gandhara relief sculpture. (3rd century A.D - National Museum, Karachi)

THE MEANING OF ARCHAEOLOGY

Presidential Address to the 12th Annual General Conference of the Museums Association of Pakistan at Peshawar, April 1962

Like most organizations in Pakistan, the Museums Association had a humble beginning. Unlike most of them, however, it continues to be a humble, almost forlorn, organization. It has no fixed address. Its headquarters are located wherever the headquarters of whoever is the Secretary for the time being may happen to be located for the time being. It has no whole-time staff, not even a messenger. In the old days, it used to receive a grant of Rs. 8,000 which was apparently considered to be on the high side and was soon reduced to Rs. 2,000. Only in the current year has the Government recognised the existence of the Association by giving it a special grant of Rs. 10,000.

In the face of handicaps such as these, it is a matter of surprise, no less than satisfaction, that the Museums Association should have survived at all. And it has not only survived, but also given public proof of its existence year after year by holding annual sessions like this, where valuable papers have been read, valuable contributions made in the sphere of archaeology and museology, and programmes of work prepared in the hope of implementing them during the course of the coming year. Nor is that all. The Association has continued, through the years, to publish a Journal of its own, the latest issue of which is before us today. One is tempted to ask how this organization has managed to live under such untoward circumstances. The answer lies in the ceaseless effort and unshakable devotion of those who have worked for this Association and kept its flag flying. They have come almost invariably from among the professional archaeologists of the country and mostly from among the members of the Archaeological Department. And if there is one name, more than any other, which deserves to be mentioned, it is that of Mr. M.A. Shakoor, our outgoing General Secretary, who has served the Association continuously for the first eleven years of its existence, and whose tireless work and unflinching loyalty to the institution entitles him to our lasting gratitude and affection.

But even when the survival of this Association has been explained in terms of the tenacious efforts of devoted enthusiasts like Mr. Shakoor and the officers of the Central Archaeological Department, the question still remains: Why should Museums and the Museums Association have lacked sympathy and support in the way they have? Whatever we may say of Government assistance, the fact

35

remains that Government is the only source from which assistance has come. The interest of the public is conspicuous by its absence. It is not that private individuals are too poor to help ; there is, as a matter of fact, plenty of wealth in the country seeking ways and means of expending itself. Nor are the requirements of an association like ours of any frightening magnitude. Oliver Goldsmith once said that half the nakedness of the world can be covered by the trimmings of the veil. One might say today that if the *nouveau riche* of Pakistan could forego the pleasure, say, of playing host at one big party once a year at one of our big hotels, they could save enough to support an organization like the Museums Association in comfort for a whole year. It may not, of course, be entirely fair to say that the rich ones of this land, whom God has blessed with so much wealth in so short a time, are not alive to philanthropic causes. Indeed, some of them have already made worthy contributions to the cause of education and public health. It might therefore be unfair to blame them without casting a close look at the Museums themselves, to see whether all is really well with them.

The Museums in Pakistan are largely those of history, art and archaeology. The Museums at Mohenjo-daro, Harappa, Taxila, Peshawar, Lahore, Dacca and Rajshahi all fall into one or the other of these categories. The Central Government has a programme of construction of a number of Museums. There will be the National Museum at Islamabad, a Central Museum at Karachi, and site museums at Swat, Bhambore, Umarkot, Comilla, Paharpur and other places. An ethnographic museum is planned at Chittagong. Some of these are already nearing completion. An Army Museum has recently been established at Rawalpindi.

The Central Government has sponsored and is maintaining most of these Museums, and it is only fair to say that the Central museums are far and away the best in the country. The fact remains, however, that our Museums lack modern techniques and facilities. There is a shortage of display space; the lighting arrangements are poor ; there are no guide books except in one or two cases (we are grateful to Providence that Sir John Marshall was spared long enough for him to revise his *Guide to Taxila* for us) ; picture cards are not available everywhere ; and there is hardly any staff to conduct museum tours.

National Museum, Karachi

Lahore Museum

Again, the museums in this country are still regarded as places of amusement rather than education. The exhibits are not arranged in such a way as to illustrate the progressive evolution of cultures or the rise and fall of civilizations. In advanced countries, the establishment of museums has now come to be regarded as an integral part of the educational process, and it is a pity that we in Pakistan are lagging so far behind in this field. Take a place like the Ford Museum in Greenfield Village near Detroit. It illustrates the development of transport. One begins by looking at the most primitive means of transport used by man in the early stages of his career on earth, and then one goes on to the more complicated vehicles that emerged from time to time over the centuries. At the end of it all, of course, one comes to the first Ford, and then to the later models. No amount of text-book reading or academic lecturing could bring before our eyes the whole panorama of transport development as this one Museum does. And this is not the only case of its kind; there are many other examples.

If we in Pakistan are to adopt the idea of the museum as a medium of education, there will have to be many more museums and those we have will have to undergo drastic changes. The exhibits will need to be arranged in an understandable order of progression, and their descriptions will have to be simpler and fuller. And we shall have to have science museums, museums of natural history, industrial museums, children's museums, and numerous other types of museums which may serve as educational guides to various age-groups of our population in various walks of life. This cannot happen unless museums, instead of being regarded, quite unjustly of course, as an isolated phenomenon representing the mental peculiarities or aberrations of their collectors and curators, become a nationwide movement and part of the educational campaign itself. Certain types of museum can best develop only in this way. For instance, it would be reasonable to expect that a museum of natural history would develop best as part of the biological faculty of a university, or that children's museums could yield maximum advantage if they were attached to schools.

I was delighted to hear from the Vice-Chancellor this morning that a Faculty of Archaeology and Museology has been set up in the Peshawar University. I hope other Universities in our country will follow this excellent example.

The paucity of museums in Pakistan is all the more disappointing since this country is extraordinarily rich in museum material. We have, in East Pakistan, rich remains of the Hindu, Buddhist and Muslim periods. Paharpur has a very large Buddhist Monastery and Stupa, Mahasthangarh has Hindu and Buddhist relics and Mainamati has very fine Buddhist remains. The Muslim monuments include the Lalbagh Fort, the Satgumbad Mosque and Bibi Pari's tomb at Dacca, the Chota Sona Mosque at Gaur (Rajshahi) and the Satgumbad Mosque at Bagerhat. In West Pakistan, we start with the relics of the Old Stone Age in the Soan Valley, the Baluchistan cultures where we see the beginnings of farming, the Amri Culture, the Kot Diji Civilization (which may or may not be an earlier phase of the Indus Valley), the triumphant route of Alexander, the period of the Kushans and others, and, most glorious of all, the Muslim period. I shall not attempt to speak about this last in detail but it might be relevant to mention the Grand Trunk Road of Sher Shah, the father of the National Highway system in this Sub-continent and probably the greatest man who ever sat on the throne of Delhi. Some parts of the original road can still be seen behind the Nicholson Monument on the way from Rawalpindi to Taxila. In Lahore, you have one of the largest mosques in the world, the Badshahi Mosque; and other monuments like Jehangir's Mausoleum and the Shalimar Gardens which rank with the best and most important anywhere. Multan has the Rukn-i-Alam Tomb and other monuments. And then we come to Sind which, like the North-West Frontier, is fabulously rich in archaeology, and where we have Amri, Kot Diji, Mohenjo-daro, Bhambore—all of them. If we are to believe Professor Kramer, Sind is the same as Dilmund, the earthly Paradise of the Sumerian imagination. And for us Muslims, Sind is the most sacred soil in this part of the world, for it is more than probable that here the Companions of the Prophet and the Companions of the Companions came. And whenever we walk the burning sands of the Sind desert, let us not forget that we might be following in the footsteps of those great men who knew the greatest man of all time!

Nor need we be ashamed to talk about the wealth that is already housed in our Museums. The National Museum which at present subsists on a make-shift basis in Karachi, has a unique collection of objects from Kot Diji and the Indus Valley Civilization, a remarkable selection of Gandhara art, (that Graeco-Buddhist art which had its beginning in the Peshawar region itself), a number of fine Hindu sculptures, and a priceless collection of the Muslim Period. We have a few thousands of original manuscripts and documents, miniature paintings, pottery ranging from the eighth century onwards, metal objects, glassware, astrolabes, fabrics and garments. The coins in the National Museum cover a wide range and include those of the Greek, Hindu, Muslim and British periods. The manuscripts include such rarities as the Diwan of Dara Shikoh, which is the only known copy so far in the world. Among documents, we have a *farman* of King Balban of the Slave Dynasty, one of the oldest documents of the Muslim period in India. The coins include one of Abdul Malik bin Marwan, the Omayyad Caliph, dating back to the year 74 of the Hijra, which again is unique. The fabrics include some belonging to the Buwaihid period, which have been studied by the French Scholar, Gaston Wiet[1].

Tomb of Shah Rukn-i-Alam, Multan

1. G. Wiet, *Soirees Persiennes*, Cairo, 1948.

The pottery includes pieces from the famous collection of Sir Eldred Hitchcock, about which Arthur Lane of the Victoria and Albert Museum has written a book.

We also have, in the National Museum, the Sikh Collection, recently acquired from the estate of Princess Bamba, a granddaughter of Maharaja Ranjit Singh himself. This again is unique.

Sindhartha fasting. This piece of Gandhara Sculpture is renowned for its superb and forceful realism expressed in face and body. 4th Century A. D. (Lahore Museum)

The other Museums are not too poor either. The Dacca Museum has invaluable Pala Sculptures and objects of the Muslim period, the Virendra Museum at Rajshahi has one of the world's finest collections of Buddhist and Hindu manuscripts and sculptures. The Central Museum at Lahore has the world-famous 'fasting Buddha'; the Peshawar Museum has priceless riches in Gandhara art, and the Taxila Museum has a variety of treasures ranging over a thousand years of history.

Having indulged in this brief reference to the archaeological and museum wealth of Pakistan, we are still left with the original problem, namely, that the number of museums is not enough, that museums other than those of history, art, and archaeology need to

41

be built and all the museums that are, or are to be, must be looked after properly.

The time has come, in my view, when this Association, with all its short-comings, must attempt to extend its sphere of activity and make concrete contributions to the development of museums. The first suggestion that comes to my mind is one which has been a favourite with my friend Mr. Shakoor and which we have, to our great regret, not found ourselves in a position to implement so far—that is, a training course in museology for a period of, say, three months, for curators and would-be curators of museums to be conducted under the auspices of the Museums Association and with the help of the Archaeological Department and other agencies concerned. The course should cover important aspects of museology and particularly museum administration, and should take account of the specialized branches of knowledge which are indispensable to a curator. The successful completion of the course should be recognised by the grant of a certificate.

The second suggestion is that the Association should try and prepare small booklets, written in simple, clear language and well got-up, on Pakistan's cultural treasures. These should serve the needs of the layman, the student and the tourist. If we could have booklets prepared, they would go far to popularise museums in this country and to acquaint the foreign visitor with the cultural wealth of Pakistan.

I would also like the Association once again to urge the Government and other agencies concerned, to improve the conditions of service of the staff of Museums. At present they are sustained mainly by their professional enthusiasm, but they and their famililies require something more by way of material suppott. In the C e n t r e, I think the Archaeological Department and the Central Museums Department should be staffed by a Class I Service at the top. That would mean improvement all round.

I spoke a short while ago of our cultural treasures. It is usual to speak of them as our cultural heritage. Here I would like to sound a note of caution. When, for example, we speak of Mohenjo-daro as part of our cultural heritage, what we mean is that the remains of the Mohenjo-daro Civilization are located in our territory, and we can readily study them. But although we accept this as part of our history, it does not follow that we accept it as part of our culture. It would be a bold Pakistani, for instance, who would wish our womenfolk to adopt the free and easy ways of the dancing girl of Mohenjo-daro. Again, shall we make a hero of the priest-king? For all we know, this dignitary was a sun-worshipper, and we Muslims certainly know better than to worship the sun. On the other hand, the town planning technique one finds in the remains of Mohenjo-daro city is worthy of our admiration. We should do well to emulate it and if possible to improve upon it. Similarly, the Mohenjo-daro sewerage system is something which it would do a great deal of good to our cities to copy. In other words, we must pick and choose in the light of standards set before us by Islam. Pakistan came into being as a result of the desire of the Muslims in this part of the world to live their own life in their own way, and nothing in the archaeological and cultural remains of past civilizations that lie in our territory, much as we might admire such remains and much as we might feel grateful for their existence, should deflect us from the main purpose for which Pakistan was fought for and won.

Having said this, let me say another word or two. Much of what I have said about the Mohenjo-daro relics applies to the relics of the Muslim period. When we see a beautiful Persian manuscript or look upon a sublime piece of Mughal architecture, do not let us be misled into ancestor-worship. Our ancestors, be they Muslim or non-Muslim, did a number of things, some of them good, some of them not so good. We should study everything, good or bad, but we must always pick and choose.

The study of the past is incumbent on a Muslim. The Quran invites our attention again and again to the events of by-gone days and the lessons that they convey. It asks us to think and reflect upon the fate of *gloria mundi*, and see how the mighty ones of old, who were drunk with the plenitude of power in their day, are now fallen and forgotten:

كَمْ تَرَكُوا مِنْ جَنَّاتٍ وَعُيُونٍ وَزُرُوعٍ وَمَقَامٍ كَرِيمٍ

وَنَعْمَةٍ كَانُوا فِيهَا فَاكِهِينَ كَذَلِكَ وَأَوْرَثْنَاهَا قَوْمًا آخَرِينَ

فَمَا بَكَتْ عَلَيْهِمُ السَّمَاءُ وَالْأَرْضُ وَمَا كَانُوا مُنْظَرِينَ

43

How many were the gardens
And springs they left behind,
And cornfields—
And noble buildings,
And wealth (and conveniences
Of Life), wherein they
Had taken such delight !
Thus (was their end) !
And We made other people
Inherit (those things) !
And neither heaven
Nor earth shed a tear over them: nor were
They given a respite (again).[2]

Nor is the rise and fall of nations a mere accident. Were it so, it could teach us nothing. According to the Quran, there is a moral order that governs the Universe. There is a moral purpose which runs increasingly through the ages ; nations are destroyed when they walk the earth in pride and sin against the laws of God :

الم يروا وكم اهلكنا من قبلهم من قرن مكناهم فى الارض مالم نمكن لكم
واسرسلنا السماء عليهم مدرارا او جعلنا الانهار تجرى من تحتهم
فاهلكناهم بذ نوبهم و انشأنا من بعدهم قرنا آخرين

See they not how many
Of those before them
We did destroy?—
Generations We had established
On the earth, in strength
Such as We have not given
To you — for whom
We poured out rain
From the skies in abundance,
And gave (fertile) streams
Flowing beneath their (feet) :
Yet for their sins

---

2. The Quran, Vol III, XLIV. 25-29, page 1348.

We destroyed them,
And raised in their wake
Fresh generations
(To succeed them).[3]

By trying to understand the moral order of the Universe and its workings we come nearer to the inner purpose and intention of the Quran. And this we can do best by studying the remains of dead civilizations that lie around us. And as we pursue our reflections, we see another great truth dawning upon us, the truth that everything we see is mortal. Only He who is Ever-Alive and Ever-Alert remains, the rest are all birds of passage :

كل من عليها فان ويبقى وجه ربك ذو الجلال والاكرام

All that is on earth
Will perish ;
But will abide (forever)
The Face of Thy Lord—
Full of Majesty,
Bounty and Honour.[4]

Or as the English poet, Shelley, puts it :-

The One remains, the Many change and pass;
Heaven's light for ever shines, earth's shadows fly.

It is the flight of these earthly shadows that archaeology and museology invite us to witness, and the more we think upon these transient forms flitting across the stage of history, the more we understand the message of the Quran.

And while we are talking of museums, is not Creation itself a museum? Is it not a museum where everything is unique, where no human being is like any other human being, where no blade of grass is a replica of another blade of grass, where even a grain of sand is different from every other grain of sand? Are not our little museums but pale shadows of the Great Museum around us, this Museum made by the Great Curator in which we live and move and have our being?

---

3. The Quran, Vol I, VI. 6, p. 290
4. Ibid., Vol III, LV. 26-27, p. 1475

to the Badshahi Masjid, Lahore built by the Emperor Aurangzeb. The gateway is elaborately decorated with framed and carved on all its facades. Its four square minarets are surmounted by red sandstone pavilions topped with white marble cupolas. 1673-74 *A.D.*

Through an arch of the Badshahi Mosque, Lahore is visible the tower commemorating the historic resolution of 23rd March 1
which demanded the creation of Pakistan.

THE LESSONS OF HISTORY

Presidential Address to the 14th *Annual General Conference of the Museums Association of Pakistan at Lahore, March* 1964

As far as I know, this is our first independent annual meeting in Lahore. It is a change from the days when we used, so to say, to enjoy the company of the Historical Society of Pakistan, and were, indeed, functioning under their benevolent care.

I am happy to think that we are meeting in this ancient city which, in its long and romantic career, has been the witness of so many historical events and has watched the rise and fall of so many cultures and civilizations. Lahore has seen the Aryan incursion, the Greek invasion, the Hindu and Buddhist dominance, the thousand years of Muslim glory, the century of British dominion and, finally, the emergence, seventeen years ago, of this Pakistan of ours as a Sovereign Independent State. The future is in the hands of the Almighty, but we hope and pray that it will be greater than the past.

The origin of this historic city is shrouded in mystery. There is a belief, largely mythological in character, that it was founded by Loh or Lava, a son of Rama Chandra, the great hero of the Ramayana, from whom it is said to have derived its name. In the beginning, the city was variously referred to as "Lohawar", "Lahawoor", "Lahnoor" and "Lahanoor", but after some time it finally settled down to its present name of "Lahore", the name we know and cherish. The excavations recently carried out by the Archaeological Department in the Lahore Fort take the story as far back as the Gupta period, in the fourth century of the Christian era, but there is no knowing whether the myth of Loh may not, on further research, turn out to be historical fact after all. In any case, whatever the age of Lahore, there is little doubt that even though it was not the first Muslim capital in this Sub-continent, it was here that Indo-Muslim culture had its birth. One can still hear the plaintive voice of Masud Sa'd Salman pining away in Naishapur for his beloved city, the City of Heart's Desire :

نگار من به لهاور و من به نیشاپور

My sweetheart is in Lahore,
While I languish in Naishapur.

The beautiful and talented Empress Nur Jahan whose last remains, like those of her illustrious husband, are enshrined in this great city of ours, is said to have paid a tribute to Lahore which is as

49

worthy of herself as of the city she loved so much :

لاہور اِ بجان برابر خریدہ ایم   جان دادہ ایم جنتِ دیگر خریدہ ایم

Dear as life is Lahore to me;
I have given my life to acquire a new Paradise.

Lahore has also been a centre of Sufism for ages. The mausoleum of Ali Hujveri symbolizes the pre-eminence of the city as the first outpost of Sufi teaching in the Sub-continent. In the first half of the nineteenth century it saw the rise of Ranjit Singh. In our own day, Lahore has become the "City of Iqbal", our immortal poet-philosopher, the man who is the father of the idea of Pakistan as well as its greatest exponent. It was here in Lahore, in his house on McLeod Road, that Iqbal conceived the idea of Pakistan in the late nineteen twenties, before he gave it to the world in his Presidential Address to the Muslim League at Allahabad on the 30th December, 1930. It was in Lahore again that, on the 23rd March, 1940, the epoch-making Pakistan Resolution was passed.

While speaking of Lahore, may I say what a wonderful time has been chosen for this session of the Museums Association. We are meeting in the heart of Spring; indeed, on the day of the Vernal Equinox itself. It is a time when this beautiful city renews itself in all its glory, when the trees and grass with their velvet green and the

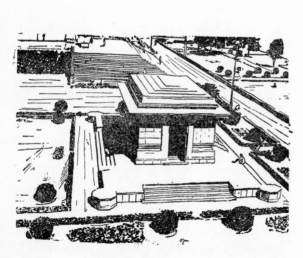

Iqbal's Tomb, Lahore

Pakistan Memorial, Lahore

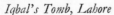

50

Alamgiri Gate of the Lahore Fort built by the Emperor Aurangzeb Alamgir 1673-74 A.D.

Jahangir's Tomb built by his son, the Emperor Shah Jahan

flowers with their infinite variety of fragrance and colour, surround the eye and overwhelm the soul. It is a time when the pulse of life beats fuller and faster; when, indeed, old men become young. Let us hope that this Museums Association of ours will imbibe the life impulse from the time and place in which it finds itself today and march forward with a new strength to greater goals of fulfilment.

Lest I succumb to the magic of Lahore, let me return to the business in hand. As President of this Association, it has been customary for me in my Annual Speeches to review in some detail the position of the various museums and museum projects in Pakistan; to take ourselves and our friends, as it were, on a sort of museological tour round the country. This has by no means been an unmixed pleasure as I am afraid I have found myself reporting lack of progress as much as progress itself. This year I thought I would make a departure from past practice and spare you as well as myself some of the avoidable frustrations of that procedure. I am tempted to do so particularly because I feel that a stage has been reached when some general observations are called for on the subject of archaeology and museology in this country. Of late, I have heard so many disparaging comments about the fruitlessness of archaeological pursuits that I have been constrained to ask myself the question: "Is archaeology or museology a waste of time?"

Speaking for myself, I would like to say that my somewhat amateurish interest in archaeology is based on two considerations.

51

In the first place, archaeology fills for me the gaps of history. I feel that the ancient historians were too snobbish or too ignorant to tell us anything about anybody except kings and queens and ministers and military commanders. It is left to the archaeologist to uncover for us the humble abode of the common man of old, and to give us an insight into his way of life. Secondly, the deeper you dig, the more connections you discover between peoples and races, and cultures and civilizations. That brings us closer to each other, and is by itself a contribution to the cause of peace and understanding in this troubled world of ours, which lives all too often under the shadow of atomic terror.

Leaving personal explanations aside, is not archaeology a branch of history, in the reading and writing of which we Muslims have always taken particular pride? As Iqbal has pointed out, the Quran repeatedly invites our attention to history and nature. From history we learn the lessons of the past. We learn how peoples and races fared in the days gone by, what made for their successes and what brought about their failures. It is important to remember, however, that the study of the past is not an end in itself. It is not the luxury of the idle mind. It is significant only because it can help in guiding us in the present. The present is more important than the past, and the future more important than the present. At the same time, it need hardly be pointed out that the present grows out of the past and the future out of the present. Thus historical research, and archaeological excavation which is a part of it, must continue to have their importance for us.

A view of the Shalimar Gardens, built by the Emperor Shah Jahan in 1642 A.D.

As regards nature, we Muslims are called upon to probe into its secrets and to harness its forces in the service of man. It is the so-called conquest of nature which gives the human being power over his environment. The dominant races of mankind have always been those whose scientists and technicians are engaged in making

52

new discoveries and inventing new technologies, not those who are out of touch with the world of matter and employ their energies on poetical composition or abstruse speculation. So it was yesterday, so it is today, and so will it be tomorrow. It is primarily scientific and technological progress that has helped men and nations to conquer the world, and the study of history, particularly of the events of the last four centuries or so, is extemely valuable to us Muslims in so far as it points to the relationship between the loss of the spirit of enquiry among us and our decadence and downfall.

It is thus clear that we in Pakistan need to learn the lessons of history once again; in particular, the great lesson of the value of scientific investigation of natural phenomena as the greatest source of power in the world. The use of that power will need to be controlled and regulated in the greater interest of humanity, and Islam, which insists on treating the whole of the human race as one unit, is a better guide for us than any man-made laws or organisations. But we have to have the power before we can think of regulating it.

As regards museums, we need not only museums of history and archaeology, but also scientific museums illustrating the triumphant march of the human mind through various fields of investigation and research. Indeed, scientific museums are even more important than museums of history or archaeology, and we should have a whole chain of them all over the country. They will help to educate our people in our great scientific heritage which we have allowed, by our own neglect, to pass into other hands that were more worthy of it. Briffault once said that modern science owed to the Muslims nothing short of its existence.[1] We have to make science our own once again, if we are to be worthy of Islam and Pakistan.

In the past, I have often spoken of the need for museums of various kinds, such as those of history, ethnography, folk art, Children's Museums and others. While all of them still have their importance, I am convinced that the greatest need of Pakistan today is museums relating to the different branches of science, particularly physics, chemistry, astronomy, biology and pyschology. Such

---

1. "The debt of our science to that of the Arabs does not consist in starting discoveries of revolutionary theories; science owes a great deal more to Arab culture, it *owes its existence*". Briffault, *the Making of Humanity* : p. 190.

museums exist in various shapes and sizes in the Departments of our Universities, but that is not enough. They need to be organised publicly for the benefit of the ordinary citizen who is often a keen and enquiring layman and more interested in scientific knowledge than we allow him or ourselves to suppose. While the Government has a responsibility in this matter, the public has even more. In particular the wealthier among us could hardly find a better object for their undoubted philanthropy. May I hope that they will give some thought to this suggestion.

As I promised earlier, I do not wish to trouble you this year with a detailed account of the various Museums in Pakistan. Nonetheless, I think I have to point to certain general requirements which are more or less common to all of them. In the first place, there is the problem of cataloguing. There is hardly a museum in Pakistan which has even a complete hand-list of its objects, leave alone a proper catalogue such as that of Rieu or Blochet. In the absence of a properly descriptive catalogue, the manuscripts, coins, paintings, pottery, sculptures and other objects that are housed in a museum have little meaning for the public whom they are intended to educate or for the research student who has to use them in the course of his research. The National Museum of Pakistan has just started preparing a cata-

The Astrolabe, the oldest existing instrument for taking the altitude of heavenly bodies, was invented by the Greeks in the second and third century B.C. The Arabs developed it on a scientific basis and it was from them that the west learnt its use. The Astrolabe displayed here was made at Lahore by the renowned mathematician Muhammad Muqim at the court of Shah-Jahan in the year 1639 A.D. (National Museum, Karachi)

logue of its manuscripts with the help of Maulana Niaz Fatehpuri, a renowned literary figure of the Indo-Pakistan Sub-continent. So far, notes on nearly two thousand manuscripts have been completed. This, however, is only the beginning of the task, most of which still lies ahead. It is necessary that all museums should undertake the work of cataloguing where it has not been done and to revise and amplify the existing catalogue where this is necessary.

There are no proper laboratory facilities for our museums. The nucleus of a chemical laboratory that exists in the Archaeological Department needs to be expanded and modernised, to enable it to undertake jobs relating to the dating, analysis and preservation of the whole range of museum objects. This means not only more equipment but also more trained personnel. The laboratory has to be considerably strengthened if it is to serve the number of museums already in existence, apart from those to be established in future. It would, of course, be best if, instead of the one laboratory we have at present in the Department of Archaeology, all important museums could be provided with chemical laboratories of their own. Any delay in this matter may, I fear, result in the loss of a number of objects, quite a few of which are already deteriorating, and the scientific treatment and preservation of which is a matter of some urgency.

The training of museum personnel inside the country could be organised by the National Museum of Pakistan, and the help of UNESCO and other international bodies could be sought for arranging training in foreign countries. The Museums Association could take an active interest in organising this programme, although they are unfortunately not in a position to help with funds.

The standards of maintenance and display, and of museum administration in general, vary with different museums. It would be desirable to have a regular inspection of all museums in the country carried out by an Inspectorate, whose personnel may be trained by the Central Government to meet not only their own requirements but also those of the Provinces. The Provinces may employ these Inspectors in their service to inspect provincial and local museums and submit reports to the Provincial Government. It is only by constant supervision over the work of museums in this country that we can hope to maintain and improve our standards.

55

In the end I must ask your indulgence if I repeat a platitude I have inflicted on the victims of these speeches from year to year. In Pakistan, we need better museums and more and more of them, particularly scientific museums, and museums of history and archaeology. They are an important medium of education and should be regarded as part of the educational programme just like primary and secondary schools. We should not be content with a few big museums in a few selected places in the country. Museum education needs to be diffused and dispersed in all parts of the country and among all sections of the population like the benefits of economic development. Even if we had one medium-sized museum for every million persons in Pakistan, we should need a hundred museums all over the country. Nor can one museum for a million people be regarded as an exaggerated demand. Indeed, it will barely touch the fringe of the problem, and the real job will still remain to be done.

Lastly, without wishing to go into any meticulous detail, may I be permitted to express the hope that the Third Five Year Plan will make adequate provision for the development of museums in this country. I do not wish to say anything about the provision of Rs. 39 lac for Museums in the Second Plan but it is clear that if the requirements of museum expansion and improvement are to be properly met, the allocation of anything less than one crore of rupees, exclusive of the provision for the National Museum at Islamabad, would hardly be adequate. I venture to submit the suggestion for the consideration of the authorities concerned. I might add that, apart from their educational value to our own people, museums are a profitable medium for the promotion of tourism, and even the financial pundits may find some consolation in the possibility of earning foreign exchange through them.

*Terracotta lion. (10th century A.D.
—Mainamati Site Museum)*

A view of Excavation at Paharpur, East Pakistan (8th Century A.D

Terracotta plaque depicting dancing girls and a piper. 1706 *A. D.—(Dacca Museum).*

A MUSEUM OF NATIONAL HISTORY

Presidential Address to the 11th Annual General Conference of the Museums Association of Pakistan at Lahore, April 1967

It has been my privilege to speak from this platform year after year. I have been making reports, surveys, observations and suggestions, and have often tried the patience of my friends in the process. This year I want to put forward only one idea, the one that is uppermost in my mind at the moment. I propose that a Museum of National History be set up in the country.

In the past there have been suggestions from time to time for a Museum of National Liberation representing the various stages of our freedom movement. Mr. Naqvi, the Superintendent of our National Museum, has sponsored the idea brilliantly in a recent article, and I think there is a great deal to be said for his proposal. I feel, however, that a Museum of National Liberation would be more significant if the historical background of Muslim rule in the Sub-continent, the decline of which is the origin of our freedom movement, is properly illustrated. A Museum of National History would set off a Museum of National Liberation to advantage. If we were to concentrate attention on the period of our political subjection alone, we might overlook the fact that we have been the rulers of this Sub-continent, and had our rise before our fall. Secondly, unless the history of our rule and the magnitude of our achievements are fully and properly projected, we might give undue importance to the days of our decline and decay. After all, we Muslims have ruled the Sub-continent for over a thousand years, as against the British who were here for less than one fifth of that period. We have to recount the story of a people who have been great in their ideas and achievements, who have filled the largest place in the history of this part of the world, who, as time went on, were tempted into ease and luxury, who developed weaknesses of organization and character and were punished with loss of freedom. It is the story of this people who, after years of struggle and sacrifice, have regained their independence and are now marching ahead with a strong will and a firm step. This story can best be told by a Museum of National History.

The main purpose of a Museum of National History would be to build up historical perspective by illustrating the most important events and achievements of each historical period, in order to reconstruct the political, economic and cultural background of Pakistan. It will be necessary not only to speak of military conquest and defeat but also of the way that the life of the people, both ruler and ruled, was built up and sustained in the economic and cultural sphere. We shall have to illustrate the development of industries, the promotion of learning, the system of justice and the system of administration and communications. What has to be aimed at is a strong and clear outline of the main aspects of Muslim dominion over this Sub-continent. Culture is a particularly important aspect of the presentation, for Pakistan itself represents essentially the struggle of Muslim culture to survive in this part of the world. Excessive detail has to be avoided; one must not lose sight of the wood for the trees.

In building up a Museum of National History, where do we begin? In the true sense of the word, Pakistan came into being when the first word of the Revelation came to the Prophet, even though the message did not travel to this part of the world till later. In the political sense, however, the first great event that laid the foundations of Pakistan was the conquest of Sind by Muhammad bin Qasim in 711 A.D. The Arab rule in Sind and the neighbouring territories continued for over two hundred years and is chiefly remembered for its humanity, tolerance and encouragement of talent. Islam was a clean break with ignorance, prejudice, social or racial discrimination, and any system of exploitation of man by man. It made education the common right of all men, instead of reserving it for a privileged class; it promoted the development of communications, it released trade and industry from its caste-bound traditions, and it helped the growth of prosperous cities. The egalitarian outlook of Islam attracted the people of the conquered territories. Muhammad bin Qasim himself became a legendary figure. When he was recalled and put to death, his non-Muslim subjects, the Hindus and Buddhists of Sind, wept for him and worshipped his idol. The new cities that sprang up during the Arab regime included Mansura, Mahfooza and Baiza. Science flourished. Among other things, scientific works were translated from Sanskrit into Arabic and scholars from the Sub-continent were invited to participate in research work in the scientific academies of Baghdad. A beginning was made with historiography in the Sub-continent with the *Tarikh-al-Hind Wal-Sind*, the original of which is lost and which is now known by its Persian translation as *Chachnameh* or *Fatahnameh Sind*.

With the decline of the central power of the Caliphate in Baghdad after 850 A.D., the Arab principality in Sind and beyond dwindled down to only two cities, namely, Multan and Mansurah. After a gap of nearly a century, we see Turkish warriors coming down the passes of the North West. The valiant Subuktegin, the mighty Mahmud and the determined Shahabuddin Ghori succeeded in laying the foundations of a new empire. The high-lights of this period are the humanity of Subuktegin (the story of his kindness to a deer is well known), the iconoclasticism of Mahmud, the great scholarship of Al-Biruni, the first Indologist of the world, and the emergence of Persian poetry in the Sub-continent in the ghazals of Masud Sa'ad Salman. Then we come to the so called Slave Dynasty where we have such remarkable figures as Qutbuddin Aybak, the outstanding administrator and sportsman who lost his life in a polo accident and lies buried in an obscure corner of Lahore, Muhammad bin Bakhtiyar Khalji, a general of Aybak, who is the illustrious conqueror of Bihar and Bengal, Razia Sultana, the first woman ruler of the Sub-continent, Nasiruddin Mahmud, scholar, saint and king, the great Balban who held the Mongols at bay, and that versatile genius Amir Khusro, poet, scholar, musician, mystic and courtier. We have great historical works like the *Tabaqat-i-Nasiri* and great architecture such as the Qutub Minar and the monuments around it. The Khaljis who came next produced a man of the stature of Alauddin Khalji, one of the greatest rulers of the Sub-continent, equally great as a general and as an administrator, who brought more of the Sub-continent, down to the extreme south, under his sway than has been the case with any Muslim ruler before him or after. His able lieutenant, Malik Kafur, is one of the great generals of history in his own right. Incidentally, Alauddin Khalji introduced the only successful Price Control Scheme ever tried in the Sub-continent.

The Tughlaqs came next. Among them, we have Muhammad bin Tughlaq, that man of ideas, who changed the capital from Delhi to Daulatabad, organized a major expedition against China and was the first to introduce token currency in the Sub-continent. Firoz Tughlaq, who came after him, and whose illustrious reign is celebrated in the pages of Ziauddin Barni, was not only a wise and just ruler but also one of the greatest builders and patrons of art and learning the Sub-continent has known.

After the Tughlaqs we have the Syeds and the Afghans with Sikandar Lodhi as probably the most prominent among them. Their

61

rule is a small interlude between the departure of the Turks and the arrival of their cousins the Mughals.

The Mughal rule in the Sub-continent infused a new vigour of life in our cultural history. Under the able guidance of the great Mughals the Sub-continent was knit into a well organised system of Government. Peace and stability combined with the broad vision and patronage of the Mughal rulers attracted talent from home and abroad. The happy blending of Persian and local art forms gave birth to the efflorescence of Mughal painting, art and literature, music, Mughal architecture, and other creative manifestations. The great Mughals were a galaxy of genius. We have the great Babur, wanderer, adventurer, warrior, poet and ruler, Akbar the empire builder, Jahangir the just, the great patron of the arts, Shah Jahan the magnificent, probably the greatest builder in history, Aurangzeb, the austere. It is only fair to add that during the Mughal period, if we were to judge by sheer achievement, the first place would probably have to go to a non-Mughal, Sher Shah Suri, the father of the national highway system, the postal system, and the revenue system, who did more in five years than any other ruler has done. We now come to the days of our decline. We have men like Muhammad Shah the dissolute. His son Ahmad Shah defeated Ahmad Shah Abdali at Sarhind and is probably the last Mughal to win a military victory. We have the invasion of Nadir Shah in 1739, the invasions of Ahmad Shah Abdali who defeated the Marathas in the third battle of Panipat in 1761. We also see the British power firmly established in the Sub-continent after the battle of Plassey in 1757. We then have the handing over of the 'Diwani' to Clive in 1765 by Shah Alam II. Here we enter a new phase.

Now starts our fight against the British who slowly but surely subdued the whole Sub-continent and entered Delhi in 1803 A.D. In the meantime, the realization was growing in the minds of our people that we, the rulers of the Sub-continent, had become helpless subjects of a powerful foreign ruler. This is the beginning of our struggle for freedom.

Now the rulers depart from the scene and the people are left to fight for themselves. With the exception of the ill-starred Sirajuddaulah, the indomitable Tippu Sultan and perhaps the titular Bahadur

62

Shah, the last of the Mughals, who became the symbol of the armed uprising against the foreign power in 1857, there is no other Muslim ruler who participated in the struggle.

We Muslims became the objects of distrust and suspicion by the British and the oppressive policy of the Government hastened the disintegration and decay of the Muslim community. In this hour of crisis those who guided our destiny and raised us from degradation to a sense of dignity were Syed Ahmad Shahid and his disciple Shah Ismail Shahid, both of whom fell at Balakot in 1831. Their following came from all parts of the Sub-continent, particularly from rural Bengal. Similarly the movement of Haji Shariatullah, Dudu Mian and Titu Mir transformed socio-religious conditions in Bengal. Their heroic resistance against the Hindu landlords and British indigo-planters created unprecedented awakening among the peasantry.

The "war of independence" or the Sepoy Mutiny of 1857, whatever we may choose to call it, is undoubtedly the most noticeable symptom of Muslim awakening. The failure of the so-called Mutiny set the Muslims thinking. An age of cool reasoning started. The man who was endowed with the qualities of heart and mind to guide us in this crisis was Syed Ahmad Khan, whose educational, scientific and social reform work was designed to bring us back from the obscure corner of history, where we were lurking and sulking at the time, into the main stream of events. The Madrassah at Ghaziabad, the M.A.O. College at Aligarh and the Scientific Society are important events in what was now to become the Pakistan Movement as we know it today. It is this Movement which produced Iqbal and Jinnah and led us on through the vicissitudes of political fortune to final victory and Pakistan.

I have attempted to give a brief glimpse of a Museum of National History as I think it should be. The various periods of our history will need separate galleries to be arranged in choronological order, to be illustrated with documents, manuscripts, diagrams, chronological charts, coins and paintings. It is essential to carry out research in order to procure material which may throw light on the life of the people. Such material is comparatively scarce at present. The Museum is likely to be an expensive project but it will be well worth the money.

The Museum of National History can give us a sense of identification with the great achievements of our past; it can help to bring home to us our common suffering under alien rule and the triumphant end of the common struggle for freedom. By doing so it can bring our people closer to each other and that is its greatest purpose.

In the end I would say that if the story of our rise and fall, and the rise after the fall, has anything to teach us, it is the vanity of human pride and the need for humility in the presence of history. We have to remember that what a civilization leaves behind are not feats of arms but the things of the mind and the spirit, the monuments of human skill, the masterpieces of art and literature and the achievements of science. But even the greatest civilization must perish, if it has outlived its inner vigour and lost touch with its original inspiration. This is what happened to us and has happened to others before us and after. God lets power pass from people to people, that they may think and reflect upon these changes. As the Quran says :

تلك الايّام نداولها بين الناس لعلّهم يتفكّرون

A miniature painting depicting a princess surrounded by a group of female musicians. Late 18th Century (Dacca Museum)
Reproduced from the original.

Lalbagh Fort Dacca--1678-79 A.D.

Terracotta plaque recovered from excavation at Paharpur. 8th Century A.D. (Paharpur Site Museum).

Terracotta lamp with stand from Mainamati, East Pakistan. (7th-8th century A. D.-Mainamati Site Museum)

EAST PAKISTAN—A CULTURAL SURVEY

Presidential Address at the opening of the Special Exhibition of Arts and Crafts of Bengal, at Dacca 1st March, 1964

This is, indeed, a memorable occasion, marking as it does the completion of fifty years—shall we say the first fifty years—by the Dacca Museum of its life as a public institution. It is a piece of great good fortune for us to be participating in these celebrations. Let us hope that, by the grace of God, the younger ones among us will have the opportunity, fifty years hence, of celebrating the centenary of this Museum.

Like everything else in this world, the Dacca Museum began in a small way. It was in 1912 that Lord Carmichael, the then Governor of Bengal, set the ball rolling with what must have appeared at the time as a munificent donation of Rs. 2,000 for the purpose of setting up a small museum. This was started in the Secretariat building—where the Medical College is housed at present—with archaeological specimens transferred from the Dacca Collectorate and elsewhere. The Museum was formally inaugurated in 1913 and opened to the public the following year. Shortly afterwards, it was declared eligible by the Government to receive coins under the Treasure Trove Act. It was not long before the existing accommodation was found to be inadequate for the increasing number of exhibits, and two more rooms were annexed for the purpose. Subsequently, the museum was removed from the Secretariat building, where it must have presented a somewhat unfamiliar spectacle, to the premises in the *Baradari* and the *Deuri* (gateway), which formerly formed part of the palace of the Naib Nazims of Dacca.

This is where it stands at present, except that two wings have been added to the *Baradari*, and the *Deuri* has been rented to the Asiatic Society of Pakistan.

When the Museum was opened to the public in 1914, the late Dr. N. K. Bhattasali was appointed its first Curator. He served till his death in early 1947 and was succeeded later by

Dacca Museum

Professor A.H. Dani, who was Curator till 1962, when he left for Peshawar. Since then, Professor A.B.M. Habibullah has been in charge, and it is largely to his initiative that we owe these Jubilee Celebrations. These learned and distinguished men who have served the Museum so far, can be justly proud of their work, particularly when we remember the meagre resources of men and money at their disposal. Curator Bhattasali, whose period of service was almost twice as long as that of his successors combined, deserves special mention and it is gratifying to know that the Museum Committee has decided to dedicate a Memorial Volume to him. It would certainly be a fitting tribute to the life and work of this remarkable man. It is on record that, in 1936, when he had a bare Rs. 4,699.00 in the shape of grants from various sources, and no more than a Chaprasi-bearer and a Durwan to assist him in the management of the affairs of the Dacca Museum, he had already published his valuable work on the iconography of Buddhist and Brahmanical sculptures, and his scholarly study of the coins and chronology of the early independent Sultans of Bengal. Today, when we are assembled here to express our pride and joy in this Museum and to render thanks for its achievements, it is only meet that we should do homage to the memory of one who served it so loyally and well.

The Exhibition of Bengal Arts and Crafts we are about to see is primarily designed to illustrate the evolution of culture in this part of the world in some of its important aspects. It covers the Buddhist, Hindu and Muslim periods and represents nearly two thousand years of history. During the whole of this period, and especially under the Muslims, Bengal has maintained a position of distinction and, in many ways, of leadership in the social and cultural sphere. Starting from a somewhat apocryphal tradition about the Buddha's visit to Bengal we have unmistakable evidence of Buddhist influence in the area as early as the third century B.C. It is possible that Buddhism had gained a foothold in North Bengal even before Asoka's time, but in the third century B.C., it became a part of Asoka's empire and Buddhism flourished

Miniature temple from Bangarh

in the area. We have archaeological relics from Mahasthangarh (ancient Pundranagara) such as terracotta plaques of the Sunga period, and the famous N.B.P. (Northern Black Polished) ware which would seem to indicate Buddhist influence in that period. The Pala Kings who ruled from the eighth to the twelfth century were great patrons of art and the famous Buddhist temple and monastery at Paharpur is a monument to their glory. A number of ornamental terra-cotta plaques, which originally decorated the base of the great temple at Paharpur, and which faithfully reflect the folk art of the period, are on display in the Exhibition along with a miniature temple from Bangarh, delicately carved out of a black basalt monolith. The Buddhist tradition was continued, particularly in the eastern districts of Bengal, by the Khadgas in the seventh, the Devas in the eighth and the Chandras in the tenth century. The excavations conducted recently by the Department of Archaeology at Mainamati have thrown a great deal of light on these dynasties. As an example, the Exhibition has two copper plates of the Deva and Chandra periods with royal inscriptions regarding grants of land.

Teracotta Sunga showing heavily decked bust af a female deity

In the twelfth and thirteenth centuries, Bengal witnessed a revival of the Brahmanical tradition during the short rule of the Sena kings. During this period, we find Hindu images in abundance all over the area, particularly in places like Vikrampur. The beautiful carved pillar you will see today in the Exhibition is an example, besides a number of other Brahmanical objects.

Hindu Image from Vikrampur

The art and architecture of the Buddhist-Hindu period in Bengal has a style of its own. Although, in its earlier stages, it was dominated by external influences, the genius of the people soon asserted itself and evolved new forms of expression. In the words of Professor Dani, "Along with the religion of the Buddha the art traditions of mid-India (Madhya Desa) were gradually absorbed into the growing influence of indigenous elements."[1] By this time the classicism of the Gupta period had given way to local tradition, and an illustration of the new development may be found in the terracotta and the gold-plated Manjusri of the period with its individual vitality and technique. We have in the Exhibition a small standing Buddha from Mahasthangarh (Vasu Vihara) which illustrates this period of artistic transition.

We now come to the greatest and most glorious period of the history of Bengal. Islam, with its egalitarian teaching and broad outlook, came to the world as a movement for human freedom. It broke the bounds of race and geography and sought to create a state of society in which every human being could realize the inner potentialities of his being and grow to his full stature. It was not surprising, therefore, that the influence of Islam should express itself in new manifestations of the human spirit in this part of the world. The language of the common man, which had been the victim of contemptuous indifference on the part of the privileged ranks of society and the use of which, as Dr. Shahidullah has pointed out, was taboo for religious purposes, came into its own largely through the preach-

1. Dr. A. H. Dani, *Buddhist Sculpture in East Pakistan*, Department of Archaeology, Karachi, 1959

70

Copper plate of Chandra period

Terracotta plaques at the Mainamati excavations

ing of Islam by Sufi saints. Bengali literature was born. The curvilinear roof of the humble bamboo hut of the Bengal village became a favourite motif in architecture. What may be called a Bengal School of Art came into existence. Education, hitherto the preserve of the higher classes, became the common property of the people. Roads, bridges and dykes were built; innumerable public buildings were constructed. The Muslim monuments that are still extant, such as the Golden Mosque at Lakhnawati and the Lalbagh Fort at Dacca, b e a r eloquent testimony to the glory of Muslim architecture. Trade and industry flourished and Dacca muslin and *jamdani* and Bengal silk, specimens of which are on display, became famous all over the world as some of the finest fabrics in existence. Bengal came, for the first time, into contact with the Middle East and the Mediterranean world. Sultan Ghiath-ud-Din Azam Shah (1389-1409) had diplomatic relations with China. The immortal Hafiz of Shiraz sang of Bangalah—a name which, as most scholars agree, itself belongs to the Muslim period.

Lalbagh Fort, Dacca

شکر شکن شوند همه طوطیان هند   زین قند پارسی که به بنگاله رود

The Songsters of the land of Ind shall relish
This sweet Persian that goes to Bangalah.
Incidentally, Hafiz seems to have honoured only two places in our part of the world in his poetry—Bengal and Kashmir.

زشعر حافظ شیراز می گویند و می رقصند   سیه چشمان کشمیری و ترکان سمرقندی

They recite the verses of Hafiz of Shiraz, and dance for joy—
The black-eyed ones of Kashmir and the sweethearts of
Samarkand.

72

It would take us far afield if we were to attempt, in any detail, to recount the services rendered by Muslim kings and scholars to the Bengali language and literature. Nor am I competent to deal with the subject. There are, however, certain well-known instances which one might perhaps be permitted to mention. One of the great patrons of Bengali was the learned and enlightened Sultan Ghiath-vd-Din Azam Shah already mentioned, who has received everlasting fame in one of the *ghazals* of Hafiz:

حافظ زشوق مجلس سلطان غیاث دین خامش مشو که کار تواز ناله می رود

O Hafiz, let not thy longing for the court of Sultan Ghiyath-ud-Din
Make thee silent, for thy affair will be furthered by thy lamentation.

It was under his patronage that Shah Muhammad Saghir composed his famous *Yousuf Zulaikha*, which is regarded by many scholars as the first work of the Bengali language. Sultan Shamsuddin Yousuf Shah (1474-1481) commissioned Maladhar Basu to render the *Bhagawat Gita* into Bengali and conferred the title of Gunaraj Khan on the poet. By all accounts, the reign of Sultan Alauddin Husain Shah (1493-1519), in whose time lived the great Chaitanya, was the Augustan age of Bengali literature. A large number of original works and translations were produced in Bengali at this time. The King's appreciation of Bengali literature, according to Dr. Habibullah, was so infectious that Paragal Khan, his Governor of Chittagong, emulating his monarch, has won everlasting fame by his patronage of Parameshwar, the earliest translator of the *Mahabharata* into Bengali. It is hardly necessary to multiply examples. Speaking of the patronage of the Bengali language and literature by Muslim kings, Dr. D.C. Sen has gone so far as to say that "Bengali would scarcely have got an opportunity to find its way to the courts of kings if the Hindu kings had remained independent."[2] The Muslim tradition continued into the heart of the nineteenth century. We have in this Exhibition two specimens of Puthi literature as it is called. Both these are in the Arabic script which, as is well known, was used for Bengali in the Muslim period. The largest collection of Puthi literature has come to us through the efforts of the late Maulvi Abdul Karim Sahitya

2. As quoted in A. Rahim, *Social History of Bengal*, Vol. I, Karachi, 1965.

Visharad of Chittagong.

No less important is the Muslim contribution to the literature of music in Bengal. A famous instance is the *Ragmala* of the poet Farid Allah which is the first work on the subject in Bengali literature.

The Muslim period in Bengal marks a new epoch in the history of architecture, which developed an individuality of its own and bears the stamp of this deltaic land. The Muslim rulers undertook many works of public utility. They did not confine themselves to building masjids, madrassahs or mausoleums; indeed, they paid particular attention to the construction of bunds and embankments to protect the people from the inundation of flood waters. Even the warrior-saint, Shah Ismail

Naulakha, Lahore Fort, built by Shah Jahan in 1631-32 *A. D.*

Ghazi, assisted Sultan R u k n - u d - D i n Barhak Shah (1459-1474) in controlling the floods in the v i c i n i t y of Lakhnawati. As already mentioned, an important feature of Muslim architecture in Bengal is the curvilinear roof of a number of royal buildings. This favourite motif, which is derived from the common bamboo hut of the Bengal village, even attracted the great Shah Jahan. The beautiful marble pavilion known as *Naulakha*, in the courtyard of the Palace of Mirrors in the Lahore Fort, which appears on the back of our one-rupee note, bears testimony to the Emperor's admiration for the bamboo hut of Bengal.

Speaking of the Mughal period, it is well to remind ourselves that Dacca came into prominence under the Mughals. It was Islam Khan, the Mughal Governor of Bengal, who selected Dacca in 1608 as his capital, and gave it the name of Jahangir Nagar after the Emperor Jahangir. The name reminds one of Shaikhupura near Lahore which was also named after Jahangir, although it was the nickname he bore as a boy—Shaikhu Baba—which came to be associated with this city. A number of illustrious governors followed Islam Khan. Among them, Shaista Khan is the one to whom Dacca owes most of its monuments, and Chittagong its old name of Islamabad. Prince Shuja, who was governor of Bengal for twenty-two years,

74

has also left us a number of famous monuments in Dacca and Gour.

In the field of calligraphy, where the Muslim genius found one of its most artistic expressions, Muslim Bengal has had a noteworthy contribution to make, particularly in the development of the Tughra script. The Bengal variety of the Tughra is characterized by the raised shafts of its vertical letters and the endless ringlets formed in expressing the round letters at the base. This ingenious arrangement of interlacing characters appeared to Ghulam Yazdani, the famous epigraphist, as comparable to the "Bow and Arrow". Other interpretations are the "Boat and Oar", "a Muslim congregation in serried line for prayer", or "the advance of a Muslim army in triumphant ranks."[3] We have some specimens of the Tughra in this Exhibition, and I should leave you to place your own interpretation on them.

Bengal produced the finest quality of muslin. This goes back to the Hindu period, but the fabric developed and became famous under the Muslims. The names given to some of its varieties, such as *Shabnam* (dew), *Ab-i-Rawan* (running water) and *Baft-i-Hawa* (the weave of the air) testify to their delicacy and refinement. Dacca muslin is said to have been so fine and light that a hundred yards of it could be wrapped round the head and one could still see the head underneath. This may well be an exaggeration, but it certainly looks as though this muslin was designed to reveal more than conceal.

The silkworm of the domesticated type, producing silk on a commercial scale, was unknown in the Hindu period. It was first introduced in Bengal by the Muslims.

The beautiful specimens of silver filigree work and ivory work we have in this Exhibition are typical of the delicate and refined craftsmanship of this part of the world. One of the unique items on display, which deserves more than passing mention, is the gold-embroidered ivory mat from Sylhet, representing as it does a degree of artistic excellence of which East Pakistan can justly be proud. Among other exhibits there are paintings which represent nineteenth century Dacca. These have a special interest in that one can easily identify some of the land-marks of this old city of ours as it was a century ago.

---

3. G. Yazdani, "Some Inscriptions of the Musalman Kings of Bengal," in *Epigraphia Indo-moslemica*, 1929-1930, p. 9.

This brings us to the British period and it only remains to take brief note of some aspects of the British impact on the Muslims of Bengal. After Lord Clive was granted the Diwani by the Emperor Shah Alam in 1765, the Muslims steadily lost their position in the revenue, judicial and military departments, which previously were their main fields of employment. Their educational system suffered a severe blow by the resumption, by the British authorities, of grants made by Muslim rulers to Muslim educational institutions, and their economic position was undermined further by the Permanent Settlement of 1793. This may partly explain the number of agrarian movements in Bengal in the eighteenth century, which culminated in the famous Faraizi Movement of Haji Shariatullah of Faridpur (1781-1840) and his son Dudu Mian. This movement, though originally one for religious reform, united the peasantry against the Zamindars and led to non-payment of certain vexatious taxes imposed by the latter. The Jehad Movement of Syed Ahmad Shahid (1786-1831), which was originally organized against the Sikhs but had important consequences for British rule in India, was largely fed with men and money from Bengal. The Districts of Jessore, Dacca, Faridpur, Noakhali, Sylhet and Chittagong were particularly in the forefront of the whole movement. Bengal was also prominent in the educational and social reform movement of Syed Ahmad Khan (1817-1898), in which, among others, Obeidi Suhrawardy (1834-1885) was a close collaborator. Obeidi was one of the original Directors of the Muhammedan Anglo-Oriental College of Aligarh, the founder and first Principal of the Dacca Madrassah, and a pioneer of Anglo-Muslim studies and of women's education. Among the great Muslim scholars of the nineteenth century may be mentioned Nawab Abdul Latif of Calcutta, who founded the Mohammedan Literary Society in 1863, the Rt. Hon'ble Syed Amir Ali who, with the publication of his *Spirit of Islam* in 1891, became a recognised exponent of Islam for the West, and Salahuddin Khudabukhsh, the great scholar of Calcutta, whose translations of German Orientalists and his original contributions still retain their importance.

Lastly, speaking of the twentieth century, it is Bengal, and particularly Dacca, which took the lead in the political regeneration of the Muslims of India. The historic meeting of Muslim political leaders in December 1906, the first of its kind, took place in Dacca in the

Shahbagh area, at the instance of Nawab Salimullah of Dacca. It was as a result of this meeting that the All-India Muslim League came into being and the Muslims of this Sub-continent were set on their career towards Pakistan. May I hope that some day a national monument will be raised in Shahbagh to the memory of this great event.

The nineteenth and twentieth centuries have left their own stamp on arts and crafts and architecture, and on life in general, in our part of the world. This has been the period of British and European influence, which is in evidence everywhere around us. Even during this period, the spirit of our people could not be subdued by the forces that surrounded them. That is the reason why our arts and crafts continued to possess an individuality which they retain to this day.

I have reached the end of the story that I have been trying to tell. I do not claim to be an authority on the subject with which I have ventured to deal and for which I have relied almost entirely on the work of others more competent than I. I have done so in the hope that this brief glimpse into the vista of bygone years may place the various objects displayed in the Exhibition in perspective. I crave your indulgence for any errors I may have committed in the process.

A page from the 'Aiini-i-Akbari', the great work of Abul Fazl, Prime Minister of the Emperor Akbar, which deals with the administrative and revenue systems of Akbar's time—18th century A.D.—(Peshawar Museum).

An Arabic inscript...
in **Thulth** script fr...
Mandra, district Dac...
It records the constr...
tion of a mosque in 8...
A. H. (1432 A. I...
in the reign of K...
Jalaluddin Muhamme...
(Dacca Museum).

A page from a unique copy of the Diwan (collected poems) of Prince Dara Shikoh, the eldest son of Emperor Shahjahan. (National Museum, Karachi).

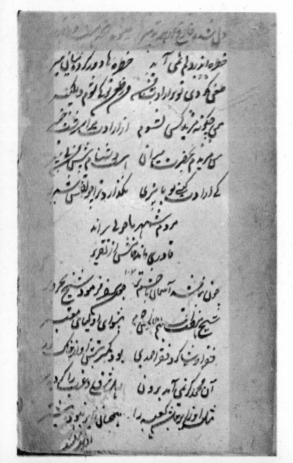

A persian inscription in Naskh on black basalt stone. It records the first Muslim conquest of Sylhet in the reign of Firuz Shah in 1303 A.D. (Dacca Museum)

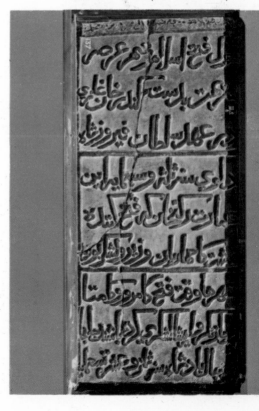

THE EXHIBITION OF ISLAMIC CULTURE

Address of welcome on the occasion of the opening of the Exhibition of Islamic Culture by Major-General Iskandar Mirza, President of Pakistan, in the Dewan-i-Am, Lahore Fort, in December 1957.

This Exhibition is the first of its kind in Pakistan, and one of the biggest anywhere at any time. The organisers had a tremendous task before them when they embarked on this venture. It was by no means easy, at such short notice, to assemble a sizeable and representative collection of exhibits from so many countries of the world. The organisers knew, however, that Pakistan had friends everywhere whose generosity and goodwill could always be counted upon. It was this knowledge and this confidence which emboldened them to go forward with their task in spite of the forbidding limitations inherent in a project of this nature. And may I add that the response that the Exhibition Committee have had from our friends abroad has more than fully justified our expectations.

This Exhibition is an attempt to represent some of the aspects and achievements of Muslim art and culture. The idea of such a representation is a challenge in itself. It is not possible to circumscribe the scope of Muslim art and culture; least of all to define its range by collecting and exhibiting a number of objects and specimens. Muslim art represents one of the greatest manifestations of the human spirit in space and time, spread over nearly fourteen centuries and embracing an enormous belt of territory from Morocco and Spain on one side to Indonesia and China on the other. Trying to bring together a fully representative collection of the many and various aspects of Muslim art in one Exhibition would, as the proverb says, be like trying to bottle up a whole river in a little jug. The organisers had, therefore, to accept the position from the very start that the Exhibition would necessarily be inadequate and incomplete in more than one respect. Their main purpose has been to bring together objects illustrating Muslim art and culture from various countries in a manner which would help to present some aspects of the greatness of that art in an abridged form and to assist in the understanding of some of its important creative trends. The specimens on exhibition are no more than a faint echo of the symphonic richness of Muslim art and culture, a mere token of the treasures that have been saved for humanity from the ravages of time and circumstance. They will have more than served their purpose if they succeed in conveying some idea, however meagre, of the glory and the grandeur that were.

The Exhibition, as you will presently see, consists of paintings, coins, manuscripts, specimens of calligraphy, arms, jewellery, inscriptions, pottery and other objects collected from the national and private treasures of nearly a dozen friendly countries. We have here some rare copies of the Quran, including one on deer skin in Kufic script belonging to the third century of the Hijra, another in the hand-writing of Sultan Ibrahim of Herat, grandson of Timur, another by the great calligraphist Yaqut Mustasimi and another by his pupil, Suhrawardy. Among other outstanding manuscripts, we have three copies of the famous Persian epic, the *Shah Nameh*. One of these, which has come from our own National Museum, is the work of the famous calligraphist, Mir Ali of Meshed, and contains beautiful miniature paintings. There is a unique copy of the *Diwan* of Prince Dara Shikoh, a manuscript of Ziauddin Barni's *Tarikh-e-Firozshahi*, which is the oldest in existence, a contemporary copy of Tippu Sultan's *Khwab Nameh* and a number of original letters including some of Muhammad Iqbal. There are valuable *Farmans*, including those of Firoz Shah Tughlaq, Sikandar Lodhi, a number of Mughal emperors including Aurangzeb, and one of Wajid Ali Shah of Oudh.

The Mughal miniatures in the exhibition largely date from the later Mughal period, but there are some outstanding ones of the earlier period as well, particularly a rare masterpiece of Akbar's time, representing a hunting scene, which has been captured by the artist with extraordinary power.

There is a large collection of rugs and carpets of outstanding importance. These include a carpet from the holy shrine of Qum, which has never left Iran before; another which is said to have belonged to Sulaiman the Magnificent; another is of Shah Jahan's time, manufactured in Lahore, and with a garden motif representing the layout of the Shalimar Gardens. There is still another which is said to have been used by Sultan Abdul Hamid of Turkey. The coins include a unique piece issued by Abdul Malik bin Marwan of the house of Omayya in the year 74 Hijra, which has a portrait of the Caliph on one side and a modified version of the Byzantine altar on the other. We also have the swords of Sulaiman the Magnificent, Sultan Murad and Sultan Bayazid of Turkey, Nadir Shah of Iran and Tippu Sultan of India. In pottery, we have some very early and rare specimens of highly glazed and painted pottery of polychrome lustre made in Iran and Iraq during the Abbasid Caliphate and earlier. We have a gold and ivory carpet from East Pakistan which is a unique specimen of

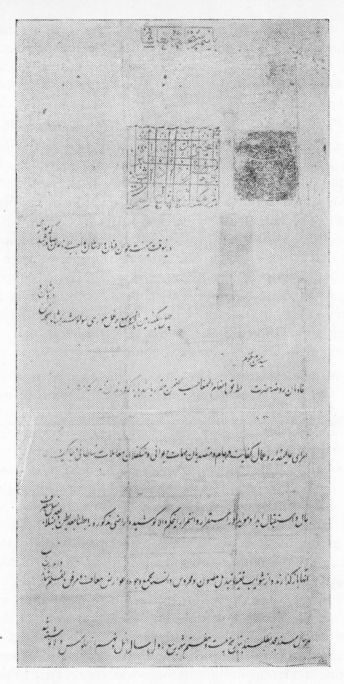

A Farman of Aurangzeb Alamgir dated 1705 *A.D.*

83

Muslim workmanship. There is a whole range of other exhibits of great value which it is hardly possible to describe in detail, but I cannot conclude this reference without mentioning Iqbal's *huqqah*, chair and carpet which, particularly the *huqqah*, have an intimate personal association with our great poet-philosopher.

We owe a debt of gratitude to Iran, Turkey, the United Kingdom, France, Germany and Italy. Here in this Exhibition are represented, among others, the India Office Library, London, the Louvre and the Musee Guimet of Paris, the Art Decorating Museum, the Bibliotheque Nationale and the National Archives of France and Museums in Teheran, Qum, Meshed and Ispahan. Some of the objects which they have been able to spare for this Exhibition are among the rarest in the world. Among the private contributors from abroad, I should like to make particular mention of Sir Eldred Hitchcock of the United Kingdom, who has sent some of the best pieces from his invaluable collection of early Islamic pottery and Mr. Joseph V. McMullan of the United States whose rare collection of rugs is one of the important items in this Exhibition.

As may be expected, a large portion of the exhibits comes from Pakistan itself. The main sources are the National Museum of Pakistan, Karachi, and the Peshawar, Lahore and Dacca Museums. The Lahore Museum possesses the richest collection of Islamic objects in this country, while the National Museum is an institution of more recent growth. Until about two years ago, there was hardly any object of the Islamic period in the National Museum although it had, and still has, the richest existing collection of material from Mohenjo-daro and a remarkable collection of Gandhara Art. During the last two years, with the help of the subsidies granted by the Government of Pakistan, a large number of paintings, manuscripts, textiles, ceramics, coins and historical documents have been collected. Visitors to the National Museum will now find in it more than a passing reminder of the period of Muslim dominion which this Sub-continent has witnessed. A selection from the Museum's new acquisitions, the possession of which entitles it to occupy an honourable place among similar institutions in the world, are on view in this Exhibition. No less significant are the contributions from the Lahore and Peshawar Archives, the Sindhi Adabi Board, the Pushto Academy and the Iqbal Academy. There are also extremely valuable contri-

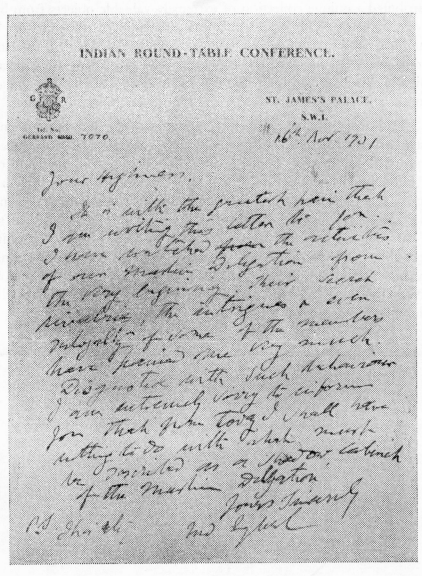

Letter from Iqbal to H. H. The Agha Khan about the Muslim Delegation to the Round Table Conference : dated 16.11.1931.

butions from private collectors, who have helped the exhibition with masterpieces from their collections. In this respect we are specially indebted to His Highness the Amir of Bahawalpur who has generously contributed a unique collection of extremely valuable objects from his private museum. Other private collectors who have responded most generously to our requests are Syed Jafer Shustri of Dacca, Maulana Abdul Aziz Memon, Sayyid Hussamuddin Rashdi, Mian Muhammad Rafi and Maulana Yousuf Binnuri of Karachi, Syed Mohammad Ramzan Shah Gardezi of Multan and Dr. Javed Iqbal of Lahore.

I am greatly indebted to my colleagues of the Exhibition Committee and particularly to Monsieur Raoul Curiel and Dr. Muhammad Baqir. Dr. Muhammad Baqir has been of great help as Secretary of the Exhibition Committee. As regards Monsieur Curiel, he has had to carry such a heavy load of work and worry for this Exhibition, and has given so much of his time and energy to it, that it is only fair to say that but for him this whole undertaking would have been quite impossible. I should also like to thank the staff of the National Museum of Pakistan, of the Old Fort and the West Pakistan Circle of Archaeology who have worked day and night in order to make the Exhibition a success.

THE ARMY MUSEUM

Presidential Address to the 13th Annual General Conference of the Museums Association of Pakistan at Rawalpindi, April 1963

It is a particular privilege for us to be in this historic city of Rawalpindi. It was here, in the Valley of the Soan, that human culture had its birth in this part of the world about half a million years ago ; it was here that the technology of stone tools was introduced. Again, it was through this region that all the invasions of the Sub-continent, except the Arab and the British, took place. This is a place where history has left its mark on almost every piece of brick and stone. And now it is the Capital of Pakistan and the centre of our political life and aspirations.

Incidentally, this is the thirteenth session of the Museums Association. Contrary to the popular superstition, I have a feeling that this is going to be a particularly lucky occasion for us all.

Looking back over the year that has passed since we met last, one can say that there has been some progress in museum development. The Bhambore and Umarkot Museums are nearing completion. The building of the Swat Museum is almost ready and display arrangements are expected to be completed before long. The new Museums at Harappa, Mainamati and Mahasthangarh and the new Ethnographical Museum at Chittagong are under construction. I was very pleased to see part of a study that is being conducted by Dr. Nazimuddin, Superintendent of Archaeology in the East Pakistan Circle, of the Murung tribe of the Chittagong Hill Tracts. This type of work has so far been done for us almost entirely by Western scholars. I hope it will now be taken up in real earnest by Pakistani scholars and research workers as well.

While on the subject, may I be permitted to say a word about the National Museum of Pakistan. It was established in 1950 and is housed temporarily in the Frere Hall building, which honours the memory of Sir Bartle Frere, the first Commissioner of Sind in the middle of the 19th Century. The Fund for the Acquisition of Antiquities for the Museum was started in 1957. The collection in the Museum now includes stone implements from the Soan Valley, fine specimens of pottery and chert implements from Kot Diji—the earliest known civilization of the Sub-continent, unique collections representing the civilization of the Indus Valley, some beautiful specimens of Gandhara art and a collection of objects from the Hindu period. A Muslim gallery has also been arranged in which extremely

89

Bhambore, excavated areas of the lower city in the foreground, the citadel in the background, and part of the defensive system in the centre.

valuable manuscripts, Imperial *farmans* and documents, specimens of calligraphy, glassware, pottery ranging from the 9th to the 15th centuries of the Christian era, coins, carpets, scientific instruments, armour and other objects of art are on display. I hope it will be possible to open the gallery to the public before long. From the Muslim period, the Museum now has, among other things, 4,000 manuscripts, 800 documents, 25,000 coins, 1,000 specimens of calligraphy and 1,000 miniature paintings. Some of these treasures, such as the *Diwan* of Dara Shikoh or the coin of Abdul Malik bin Marwan of the year 74 A.H. or the *farman* of King Ghiathuddin Balban of the Slave Dynasty, are unique. The number of rare and very rare items is too long to be recounted. It may not be an exaggeration to say that this comparatively young Museum, even though it is still very small as compared with museums in many other countries, has already entered the world class. Let us hope that as time goes on it will add substantially to its valuable collections and take its rightful place among the great Museums of the world.

Lest I be accused of painting too rosy a picture I ought to say that there is a great deal that has still to be done for Pakistan's museums. We need more and more of them, and we need them bigger, more comprehensive and better arranged. To mention one or two instances, the Lahore and Peshawar Museums still need a great deal of attention as do the Rajshahi and Dacca Museums. Particular urgency attaches to the requirements of the Dacca Museum, to which the collection of the Balda Museum has already been transferred and for which the Provincial Government has also acquired the Dinajpur Collection.

The Second Five Year Plan envisages the establishment of a number of museums some of which, as I have already said, are under

Swords, guns and other weapons exhibited in the Army Museum

construction. Others, including the proposed Central Museum at Karachi and the National Museum at Islamabad, are in the preliminary stages. The total provision for the development of museums included in the plan amounts to Rs. 39 lac. While this may be regarded as a reasonable provision for the current plan, it is quite clear that, if museums are to provide the services for which they are designed, much more will need to be done in this field than has been done so far, and the provision in the Third Plan will have to be much more substantial.

One of the most important aspects of the development of museums is their importance as a medium for education and instruction. Education is the basic requirement of Pakistan's development; it is the only safeguard of political and economic progress. And if it is to achieve its purpose, it has to be cheaper, quicker and much more common than it is today. Indeed, it must be universal. This will not be possible in the near future unless all available resources are mobilised for the cause of education. This is where museums can make a contribution. They are a very important medium of instruction and we in this country have to make use of them more and more as an aid to the educational effort. In advanced countries it is usual to see museums in schools, colleges, universities and even government departments. I remember the vivid impression which the Museum of the Board of Customs and Excise in London made on me some years ago. In this country, in a few years' time, the number of museums that will be required is likely to be completely out of proportion to what we have today. There will have to be museums of archaeology, geology, zoology, botany, history, ethnology, art, science and technology, childrens' museums and others. The sooner we embark on a proper long-term plan of museum expansion the better it will be for the cause of education. It seems to me that while the effort and expenditure involved will necessarily be spread over more than one Plan period, it would be reasonable to suggest that the provision for museums in the Third Five Year Plan should be at least double that in the Second Plan.

Speaking of museums as a medium of education and instruction, it is necessary to point out that the scope of our museums needs to be enlarged. In particular it has to be remembered that :—

(i) objects placed in museums, even in archaeological museums, need not necessarily be hoary with age. Sir Mortimer Wheeler, speaking at Karachi last year, said that archaeology was not a matter of a hundred years ago but even of yesterday. We in Pakistan would be well advised to bear his wise observation in mind;

(ii) a museum no longer consists of visual objects alone. Its scope is now audio-visual and it should contain sound and voice records as well as films; and

(iii) instead of people visiting museums and trying to extract knowledge out of labelled descriptions by their own individual effort, it is necessary to have conducted tours by scholars and expert guides. Through them, the museum should speak to its visitors instead of standing, as it were, in dignified and sullen aloofness.

May I now refer briefly to the Army Museum. I think the Army authorities are to be congratulated for setting it up, and I hope that other departments will follow their lead. This is an excellent beginning. I am sure that the Army would wish to extend the scope of the Museum beyond the British period to which it is confined at present. Our British military heritage is undoubtedly something to be proud of and to preserve. It has brought us into contact with some of the finest traditions of modern times in the matter of training, discipline and professional pride. What it has not done, and cannot do, is to provide our fighting men with a source of inspiration. For that we have to turn to the life of the Prophet and the history of Islam. That is what I may be permitted to call our spiritual L. of C. In this Museum, then, we need not only the objects of the British period, and more of them if possible, but also those of the Muslim period and the earlier periods of the history of the Sub-continent. If maps and models could be prepared of the more important battles and campaigns, they would serve to illustrate the military history of the Sub-continent in a graphic and readily understandable manner and would prove as interesting to the layman as to the professional soldier. Could the Arab conquest of Sind, including the siege of Daibul, the battle of Alore, and that master-piece of 'Q' organisation, Muhammad bin Qasim's march through the Iranian desert, be illustrated in this way?

Would it also be possible to have a systematic study of the famous battles of Indo-Pakistan history? Many of these battles disclose a marked contrast between faster and more manoeuvreable techniques of offence and heavier and less mobile forms of defence, with cavalry on the one side and elephants on the other. Battles such as those between Alexander and Porus, Anandpal of Lahore and Mahmud of Ghazna and the three battles of Panipat would be particularly interesting from this point of view. It would not be far wrong to call them the battles of the Horse and the Elephant, and to have a section of the Museum entitled *Horse versus Elephant* for such battles.

May I also suggest that another section be set up in the Army Museum relating to the battles and campaigns of the Prophet and his successors and the most decisive battles of the subsequent history of Islam. The Military Museum at Cairo has set us an example in this field. I still have a vivid recollection of the maps of Badr, Uhad and other battles of the Prophet, which I saw in that Museum some years ago. If the Army Museum could do something on these lines, it would add substantially to our understanding of the personality of the Prophet and the history of Islam.

One word more and I have done. Many of us have felt perturbed at reports which have been appearing from time to time in the newspapers about the allegedly unauthorised export of our antiquities. I hope these reports are exaggerated, and am quite sure that the matter is fully present to the mind of the authorities concerned. I also hope that such action as may be called for will be taken quickly and effectively to ensure that treasures which should adorn the Museums in this country do not find their way abroad.

THE HISTORICAL BACKGROUND OF THE RCD

Presidential Address to the 16th Annual General Conference of the Museums Association of Pakistan at Karachi, April 1966

During the year that has elapsed, a number of interesting and important developments have taken place. I would like to refer particularly to the growing relationship between Iran, Turkey and Pakistan under the auspices of the RCD. This is a momentous event. It looks as though the great dream of Muslim unity and co-operation that was dreamt by Jamal-ud-Din Afghani, Mohammad Abduh, and Mahammad Iqbal is about to come true.

The Muslim world, as a whole, is bound by common ties of religion, history and culture, but for the present I propose to concern myself with the three RCD countries.

The relationship between Iran and Pakistan goes back to pre-history. The close resemblance in the art of pot-making in the pre-historic village cultures of Baluchistan and Mohenjo-daro with that of Sialk in Iran, together with the other archaeological data recently discovered on the Makran coast and the North-west of Pakistan bear proof of cultural contact between the two countries in pre-historic and proto-historic times.[1] The pottery designs of the Bampur Valley site in South-east Iran such as humped bulls, tiny horned goats and plants with broad leaves appeared in the pre-historic sites of Pakistan, particularly at Kulli and Chanhudaro.

The net-work of pre-historic routes in Iran as brought to light by recent archaeological researches throws light on the way in which important outposts in Baluchistan and the coastal areas of West Pakistan were linked to the main arteries of communication.[2]

At the beginning of the Medic period, about 700 B.C., the people of West Pakistan and Iran were united in a common Pak-Iranian race located somewhere in the Punjab.[3]

In the Achaemenian period (521 B.C.) when the Persian empire was at its zenith, Darius (521-485 B.C.) deputed the Greek Admiral Scylan to discover the sea-route to India. This led to the conquest of Sind, the Punjab and Afghanistan and their annexation to the Persian

---

1 F.A. Khan, *Indus Valley and Early Iran*, Karachi 1964, p. 10. Also George F. Dale, "Search for Ancient Seaports," in *Expedition* Vol. 4, No. 2, 1961, p.2

2 Bahman Karimi *Pre-historic Roads In Iran*. (Persion)

3 E.G. Browne, *Literary History of Persia*, Vol. 1, p. 33. Browne, uses the words "Indians and Persians" and "Indo-Iranian", which, in the present context means "Pakistani and Iranian" and "Pak-Iranian."

empire.[4] Sind and part of the Punjab constituted the twentieth, or Indian, satrapy of the Empire, and included Taxila, where Sir John Marshall thinks the Persian conquerors founded Bhir ' Mound, the earliest of the ancient cities of Taxila.[5] Iron was introduced in Pakistan during the rule of the Achaemenids. The archaeological excavations recently conducted by the University of Peshawar at Balambat near Timargarha in Dir State have brought to light an Achaemenid settlement with the complex of a fire temple. We can also trace old Persian influences in Mauryan art and architecture. The similarities and resemblances between Achaemenid and Mauryan architecture are so marked that some of the writers have gone so far as to say that the Mauryans employed Persian architects. Above all, the agrarian measurements, mercantile weights, and measurements of roads in ancient Pakistan were all introduced under Persian influence. The Aramaic inscription of Taxila indicates the development of a common language in Iran and Pakistan during the Achaemenid period. Mani visited West Pakistan en route to Tibet and China between 242-276 A.D. on a preaching mission.[6] Vendidad (351-379 A.D.) describes "Hafta-Hendu" or Seven Rivers (the old Punjab) as one of the creations of Ahura-Mazda.[7] Persian influence in Pakistan is found in certain coins of the third century A.D. which have been discovered in the old Punjab area and bear the impression of a fire altar as in the coins of Ardeshir Babakan (d. 241 A.D.) of the Sassanid dynasty. The dress of King Vasudeva (d. 245 A.D.) on his coins is similar to the dress shown on the statue of Shapur I (d. 271 A.D.). It is also recorded that the Gupta emperors adopted the Persian hair style, and the Persian habit of riding donkeys became common among the people of West Pakistan in the Gupta period. The Asoka pillars are modelled on those of Takht-i-Jamshed (Persepolis).[8]

The Mauryan emperors modelled themselves on the Achaemenid rulers and Vincent Smith has been at some pains to point out that the Mauryans were influenced by Persia in spite of the presence of Greek

---

4 M.A. Ghani, *Pre-Mughal Persian in Hindustan* p. 6. Also E. G. Browne, *Literary History of Persia*, p. 94.

5 J. Marshall *Guide to Taxila*, p. 11.

6 Jairazboy, Foreign *Influence on India*, p. 132. Hadi Hasan, *Majmua Maqalat*, pp. 33-35.

7 E. G. Browne, *Literary History of Persia*, Vol 1, p. 35.

8 Rawlinson, *Indian Art*, p. 52.

Ambassadors, including the famous Megasthenes, at their courts. The Persian designation of "satrap" was widely used in the Mauryan empire for provincial governors and it remained current up to the fourth century A.D. The influence was, of course, far from being one-sided. For example, the game of chess was exported to Iran from Sind. So were the elephants which the Iranian King Shapur II is said to have used in the year 360 A.D. against the Romans. According to the author of the *Majma-ut-Tawarikh*, Kandabil[9] and Bahman-abad (Mansurah) were founded by Bahman in the reign of Gushtasp. The famous Bahram Gur (420-438 A.D.) married the daughter of King Shankul, a princess from West Pakistan, and Daibul and Makran passed to him as part of his wife's dowry. Bahram also asked Shankul to send ten thousand singers and dancers, both men and women, to Iran to entertain the common people of the country. Firdausi tells the story:

بزدیک شنکل فرستاد کس
چنین گفت کای شاه فریادرس

نژو ماده برزخم بر یط سوار
ازان لولیان برگزین ده هزار

He sent a messenger to Shankul,
Who said to him, O just King!
Choose ten thousand from among these "Loolian",
Choose men and women, who are adept at music.

It was the singing girls among these ten thousand who came to be known as "Loolian" in Iran. Hafiz seems to have lost his heart to them and has celebrated the experience in a famous verse:

فغان کین لولیان شوخ شیرین کار شهر آشوب
چنان بردند صبر از دل ترکان خوان یغمارا

Alas for me, these saucy troublesome "cuties"
Have plundered all patience from my heart
As though they were the marauding Turks.

---

9 *Majma-ut-Tawarikh*, p. 118.

The "Loolian", incidentally, are believed to have been from Rohri in the Sind area. Their original name is said to be "Luhrian" from "Luhri", the original name of Rohri.

In the reign of Noshirwan (531-579 A.D.) the "vina", a highly developed and delicate musical instrument, found its way to Iran.[10] Among the books translated into Pahlavi in Noshirwan's time was one concerning the Buddhist religion, which at that time was one of the main religions in West Pakistan.

The events that occurred after the advent of Islam are well known, but it may be relevant to recall that, geographically speaking, Islam came to Pakistan through Shiraz, which was the headquarters of Muhammad bin Qasim, the young general who conquered Sind in the year 93 of the Hijra. His army, which moved from Shiraz, contained a number of Persian soldiers, whose arrival in Pakistan in this victorious campaign was the beginning, however small, of our continuous contact with the Persian language. Persian could not make much headway just at the time, because the court language then was Arabic, but the seed was sown which flowered later. As we all know, Persian was the court language of Muslim rule for nearly a thousand years. During this milleneum, Iran and Pakistan came so close to each other in the cultural field that it would be difficult to separate the two.

When Humayun lost his throne to Sher Shah, he took refuge in Iran, and sought the help of King Tahmasp of the Safavid dynasty to re-establish himself in the Sub-continent. Jahangir used to address Ismail Safavi as 'brother'. There always were both Iranian and Turanian nobles at the Mughal court. The Empress Nur Jahan, "the light of the world", who was an Iranian from Tehran, was one of the most powerful influences in Mughal history.

Speaking of Iran's cultural influence, poetry, painting, architecture, calligraphy and gardening, all received their inspiration from Iran. Some of our greatest poets, like Khusru, Bedil, Ghalib and Iqbal, were poets of the Persian language. After Iqbal, the Persian literary tradition is having a revival in Pakistan.

The influence of Bihzad on our miniature painting is all pervasive. His work has been a constant source of inspiration to the artists

---

10 Hadi Hasan, ibid.

of this Sub-continent. The theme and treatment of subject, the colour scheme and the design in the art of the Sub-continent bear the indelible marks of Iranian art.

In architecture, we borrowed from Iran all the elements that are characteristic of Muslim architecture in the Sub-continent, such as the arch, the vault and the dome. The screen arch in the Masjid Quwwat-al-Islam in Delhi and in the Arai Din Ka Jhoupra in Ajmer of the early thirteenth century bear the stamp of Saljuqid Iran.[11] The Madrassah type of Masjid originally developed in Iran has its counterpart in Pakistan in the Badshahi Masjid, Thatta, and the Wazir Khan Masjid in Lahore. While studying the exquisite tile decoration in the Badshahi Masjid, Thatta, the distinguished archaeologist, Sir Mortimer Wheeler, was struck by the Persian character of the whole design.[12]

Of all the arts that developed under the patronage of the Muslims in the Sub-continent, the most sacred was Arabic writing. Arabic was for them the vehicle of the Quran, the very basis of life, religion and civilization. Here also, the creative genius of Iran was not satisfied with adopting the Kufic and Naskh scripts, which were originally evolved and developed by the Arabs. There developed Taliq and Nastaliq in Iran. Of these Nastaliq became particularly popular in the Sub-continent from the sixteenth century onwards on account of its round and flowing dictus.

In a lush green area like the Indo-Pakistan Sub-continent, the idea of a garden, walled and terraced, was almost unknown. It originated in the plateau of Iran where desert and oasis was a familiar feature of the landscape. The purpose was to break the monotony of the desert as well as to save the garden from the onslaught of the moving sands.

The Iranian type of garden, such as Char Bagh, was introduced in the Sub-continent by the Mughals. The Shalimar Garden with its three terraces, each with its own distinctive name, is one of the outstanding gardens of the world.[13]

It is clear that Iran contributed immensely in the spread of know-

---

11 Percy Brown, *Indian Architecture (Islamic period)*, pp. 9-10.
12 R. E. M., Wheeler, *Five Thousand Years of Pakistan. London* 1950. *p* 69.
13 *Cultural Heritage of Pakistan*, Department of Archaeology, Pakistan, pp. 50-1.

ledge of agriculture, pot-making, metal-work and many other pursuits that, in the aggregate, formed a more civilised style of living in Pakistan both in pre-history and history. In a word, it is impossible to study the evolution of Pakistani civilisation without reference to Iran.[14]

May we now turn to Turkey. The relations between Turks and Pakistanis go back to pre-Islamic times. In the eighth century A.D. the Uyghur Turks established an empire in Mongolia on the banks of the river Orkhun.[15] By the seventh century A.D. Buddhism became popular among them and attained the status of state religion.

The Uyghurs had close contacts with Gandhara as it was the centre of Mahayana Buddhism. There was a movement of artists from Gandhara and with the artists moved the ideas. That is why we find a large number of Sanskrit words in the Uyghur language.

In this Sub-continent the Turks were not at all unknown. In Sanskrit literature, the word 'Turk' is written as 'Turushka'. The Turks also exercised political influence on the Western part of Pakistan to a great extent. The Turkishahi dynasty with their capital at Kabul virtually ruled the greater part of Gandhara and the Punjab. The great Kushans and the Huns, who belonged to the same race, penetrated all over West Pakistan. Gandhara, the centre of Mahayana, radiated the light of Buddhism all over Central Asia. The Gandharan element can be detected in the Buddhist sculpture and literature of the Uyghurs. Buddhist influence was so dominant even during the early phase of Arab rule in Turkistan that the Muslims had to organise a net-work of missionaries in the area. The difficulties of Muslim preachers have been vividly described by the famous Lexicographer Mahmudal-Kashgari in his well-known work *Diwan Lughat-al-Turk*.[16]

From the Turkishahi period onwards, the Turks were rulers of West Pakistan and beyond. The Turkishahis were replaced by the Ghaznavids. Many Turkish tribes settled down in the Sub-continent. The Mamluks, the Khaljis, the Tughlaqs and the Timuris all were Turks. A large number of Turkish words found their place in the

---

14 Abdul Ghafur, "The Role of Iran in the Evolution of Ancient Pakistan and Civilisation," *Jam-i-Jam*, March 1967, Karachi, p. 44 *et. seq.*

15 Barthold, *Turkestan Down to the Mongol Invasion*, p. 32.

16 Muhammad Saber, "Urdu Main Turki Aur Mangoli Alfaz", *Urdu Name*, No. 13, July-Sept., 1963, pd.7-26.

vocabulary of the Urdu language, apart from the fact that 'Urdu' itself is a Turkish word. Some examples are:

اتالیق ۔ خاتون ۔ بیگم ۔ تمغہ ۔ قلی ۔ قیمہ ۔ قورمہ ۔ پلاؤ ۔ چچہ ۔ قینچی ۔ چاقو ۔ آپا ۔ باجی ۔ خان

Almost all the Mughal emperors could speak Turkish. In 1881 there were about 12000 Barlas and about 23000 Chaghtais settled in and around Delhi and Rawalpindi. Turkish, incidentally, is the only Asian language which is spoken by a considerable number of the European population in Eastern Europe, such as Finland, Roumania, Bulgaria, Greece, Yugoslavia and Albania. There are over 20 Turkish words frequently used in the *Tuzuk-i-Timuri*. Similarly in the *Humayun Nameh* of gulbadan Begum, there are more than 100 Turkish words; and so is the case with the *Ain-i-Akbari*, the *Tuzuk-i-Jahangiri* and other works. It shows how deeply Persian, Turkish and Urdu are intermingled. The Persian influence on Osmanli Turkish is too well known to need explanation.[17]

This mutual influence can easily be seen in the field of the creative arts such as architecture, painting and calligraphy. The revival of the Sassanian architectural form by the Saljuks led to the efflorescence of Muslim architecture in the 12th century. On the other hand, the Saljuki influence played an important role in the evolution of Indo-Muslim architecture in the Sub-continent. What has come to be known as Pathan architecture is predominantly Turkish in point of origin and evolution. The Turkish and Persian patterns of creative design on tile work, book-binding, carpets and calligraphy are apparent in our decorative art.[18]

The first Turk to come to Pakistan as a Muslim was Subuktegin, father of Mahmud of Ghazna, who defeated Jaipal of Lahore in the year 376 of the Hijra (986-7 A.D.)[19] Then comes Mahmud himself, with his seventeen invasions of the Sub-continent, and the Mamluk Kings of Delhi, headed by Qutb-ud-Din Aybak, the slave of Shahab-ud-Din Ghori. From the Mamluk dynasty begins, in 1206 A.D., the regular phase of Turkish rule in the Sub-continent. The Mamluks

---

17 Ibid, p. 15.
18 Percy Brown, *Indian Architecture* (*Islamic Period*,) p. 72.
19 Abu Nasr Muhammad bin Muhammadal-Tabbar-al-Utbi, *Tarikhal-Yamini*, pp. 9 and 22. Also Muhammad Nazim, *Mahmud of Ghazna, Cambridge,* 1931.

were followed by the Khaljis and the Tughlaqs, all of them Turks. These Kings included conquerors and administrators of the stature of Alauddin Khalji, who subdued practically the whole of the Sub-continent, builders and patrons of art like Firoz Shah Tughlaq, and saintly scholars like Nasiruddin Mahmud. It was these Turkish kings who kept the Mongols of Chengiz Khan out of the Sub-continent, a n d protected its culture and civilization f r o m destruction. The Mughals who ruled the Sub-continent from 1526 to 1857, with the brief interruption caused by Humayun's defeat and exile, were the first cousins of the Turks. Up to the time of Humayun, communications were open and visits were freely exchanged between the Sub-continent and Central Asia, the home-land of the Turks and the Mongols. It may be of interest to mention that it was as a result of the patronage and encouragement of the earlier Turkish kings that Persian was firmly established as the language of the court, and of culture. In particular, the best known literary and political histories, such as Aufi's *Lubab-al-Albab* and Juzjani's *Tabaqat-i-Nasiri* were written in the Turkish period.[20] Amir Khusro of Delhi, a Turk, who is probably the most versatile genius ever produced by the Sub-continent, is the product of the Turkish era. The Mughal Emperors and princes and nobles almost all of them knew Turkish. Many of them, like Babur, Humayun, Kamran, Bayram Khan Khankhanan, Abdur Rahim Khan Khankhanan, Jehangir and others wrote Turkish poetry. Even in the nineteenth century, we have Azfar Gurgani, one of the well known poets of the Turkish language.[21]

When the Muslims lost t h e Sub-continent to the British they looked to Turkey for support and protection. One of the prominent Muslim rulers who sent an embassy to the Turkish Caliph was Tippu Sultan of Mysore. Throughout the British period, the Muslims of the Sub-continent were emotionally and politically affected by the fortunes of Turkey. The Urdu and Persian poetry of the late nineteenth and twentieth centuries centred round the Caliphate. The Balkan war of 1911 was an occasion for a resurgence of Muslim feeling in favour of the Turks. Money, clothes and all sorts of other gifts flowed freely to Turkey, and a medical mission of volunteers

20 Storey, *History of Persian Literature*, Vol. 1, p. 1229.
21 Muhammad Saber, ibid.

under the leadership of the late Dr. Mukhtar Ahmad Ansari proceeded to Istanbul to offer their services. The Indian Muslims adopted the *fez* as their distinctive headwear in the nineteenth century. Along with the Turkish coat, it was part of the uniform of Aligarh College, now the Aligarh University. When the Turks under Ataturk discarded the *fez*, the Mustafa Kemal cap became the fashion instead. Many a young Muslim in the Sub-continent modelled himself on Turkish dignitaries. In the *Fasana-i-Azad*, the classic romance of Sarshar, the hero, a native of Lucknow, enters the Turkish army and becomes a Pasha. A recipient of a Turkish Honour was generally known as Effendi. We have had a famous Effendi in Karachi, the founder of the Sind Madrassah. The Hijrat Movement of 1919, and the Khilafat Movement of 1921, the former of which resulted in the exodus of about 18,000 Muslims from the Sub-continent, and the latter in a much larger number going to jail, were in the nature of a protest against the British treatment of the Turks. The Turko-Greek struggle in Anatolia after the First World War drew from Iqbal two of his greatest poems. When the Turkish forces were under pressure, and things were going bad for them, he wrote the *Khizr-i-Rah* ("The Guide"), a most moving poem full of sadness and depression, albeit with a note of hope at the end. When the Greek forces had been driven out, and Turkey was back on its feet, Iqbal wrote the *Tulu-i-Islam* ("The Emergence of Islam"), every line of which is full of a sense of triumph. The feeling for the Turks was by no means confined to Iqbal. Muhammad Ali Jauhar had gone to jail earlier for having championed the Turkish cause in an article entitled "The Choice of the Turks". Even at this distant date, the names of Enver Pasha and Ghazi Mustafa Kemal are famous in song and story, even in the countryside. It was common in the nineteen twenties to hear young girls in the Punjab villages sing:

غازی انور پاشا موڑ مہارو سے

O Ghazi Enver Pasha, turn thy horse towards us.

or:

غازی مصطفٰی کمال وے تیریاں دور بلائیں

O Ghazi Mustafa Kemal, may all thy troubles vanish!

In Bengali too, Nazrul Islam has written admiringly of Mustafa Kemal.

The unprecedented welcome that Rauf Bey, the hero of the "Hamidiyya", or Halide Edib Hanum, the famous Turkish politician and writer, received when they visited Pakistan territory showed the affection in which every Turk was held, irrespective of the position he had in Turkey.

Pakistan's cultural links with Iran and Turkey are not confined to any particular area. Under Muslim rule, the whole of the Sub-continent was integrated into one cultural unit, in spite of the fact that at various times, a number of independent and semi-independent principalities were in existence in various parts of it. For example, the independent Sultans of Bengal, who ruled for nearly two centuries, had Persian as their court language.[22] Ghiathuddin Azam Shah, one of the greatest of these Sultans, is said to have invited Hafiz of Shiraz to Bengal. Hafiz could not come, but in reply to the invitation he sent the King a famous ghazal, which now forms part of the Diwan.

The independent Sultans of Bengal not only patronised local talent and promoted local languages and literatures, but also maintained a strong cultural link with the rest of the Sub-continent, and with the Muslim world as a whole.[23]

The old names of many of the important cities of East Pakistan have a Persian ring about them. For example, Chittagong was known as Islamabad, Sylhet as Jalalabad and Dacca as Jahangir Nagar. The History of Chittagong, published in the last century, was written in Persian by Hamidullah, under the title *Tarikh-i-Islamabad*. Some other examples are *Tarikh-i-Bangala* by Ghulam Sarwar and the *Ahwal Gaur Wa Pandua* by Shyam Prashad. When Munshi Abdul Ali of Chittagong, who lived in the nineteenth century, wanted to write a book for his only son, he chose Persian as his medium of expression out of the five languages he knew, including his mother tongue Bengali. Abdul Ali has said that Persian was used in earlier times in Bengal almost like a mother tongue. There are a number of other important works, chiefly historical, written in the last century or earlier in East Pakistan in the Persian language. The develop-

22 A. Rahim, *Social History of Bengal*, pp. 19-21.
23 A. Rahim, ibid.

ment of the Bengali language under the patronage of Muslim rulers owes much to the benign influence of Persian.[24] The development of communications helped cultural integration. Sher Shah's famous Grand Trunk Road started from Sonargaon and continued up to Peshawar. Under the Mughals, when Bengal was a province of the empire, it had a number of well known governors, such as Prince Shuja, brother of Aurangzeb, Shaista Khan, Mir Jumla and others who served the cause of administration as well as that of culture.

As regards East Pakistan's links with Turkey, it is sufficient to recall that Bengal was conquered by the Turkish general, Ikhtiar-ud-Din Muhammad Bakhtiar Khalji, with the help, incidentally, of eighteen horsemen. Bakhtiar Khalji had already conquered Bihar with two hundred men. There are some Sher Shah cannon in the Dacca Museum which show that Sher Shah employed Turkish workmen to improve the make of his guns.

It is not my purpose to go into any further details. I just wanted to indicate how deep the roots are of the relationship between Pakistan, Iran and Turkey. We in Pakistan are proud of that relationship. The Turks and Iranians are not foreigners to us. They are part of us, and we are part of them. When Tennyson welcomed the Danish Princess Alexandra on her marriage to Prince Edward, later Edward VII of Great Britain, he reminded her of the close kinship of the British race with the Danes. "Saxon and Norman and Dane are we," he said. We can say something similar: Turks, Iranians, Afghans, Mughals and Arabs all have entered into the composition of the Pakistani people just as Saxons, Danes and Normans constitute the British race. We Pakistanis are Turks, Iranians, Afghans, Arabs and Mughals—all of them—even though racial origins are hardly significant for us as compared with the common culture and outlook of Islam we share together.

May the friendship of Iran, Turkey and Pakistan grow with the years and bring its benefits and blessings not only to our three countries, but also to the Muslim world and to humanity as a whole.

---

24 *Ibid.*

BUDDHISM IN PAKISTAN

Speech at the Buddha Purnima at Karachi, May 1967

I am deeply honoured by your kindness towards me today. I am particularly touched by the fact that you have asked me to share your happiness on this important and auspicious occasion, the Buddha Purnima, which commemorates the birth, enlightenment and death of the Buddha. The honour you have done me today comes to me through your generosity and not from any merit on my part. I am grateful to you.

Nor can I hope to thank you adequately for the kind words you have said about me. If I have tried to render any service to the cause of education, it is because I feel that education is the one point of breakthrough for our development, be it economic, political or cultural. If I have taken interest in Pakistani culture, it is because I admire it. Pakistani culture is a garden of many flowers, and it is all the more beautiful and all the more fragrant for its variety. The flowers are many, but the garden is one, and I love that garden.

I come to you as a Muslim who finds a number of things in Buddhism to admire. In the first place, there is the Buddha himself, who is to us one of the greatest men that ever lived. He is great because, like Muhammad, he concerned himself with the whole problem of life, and thought of the human race as one. He made no distinction between man and man, and could not bear to think of anything so inhuman as the Caste System. The Sakyamuni, as he is often called, was deeply pained by the phenomenon of human suffering and came to have profound compassion for humanity. He devoted himself with all the sincerity that the human soul is capable of to the quest for a remedy for human ills. And when the moment of enlightenment came, when Prince Siddhartha became the Buddha, it brought him a message for all mankind. That is the point about any great message; it has to be universal. And there is a universality of approach, a catholicity of outlook that is visible in all the manifestations of Buddhism.

Like Christ and Muhammad after him, Buddha wanted peace on earth and goodwill among men, a message that is vital to human beings in the troubled world of today.

Like Muhammad, Buddha always insisted that he was only a human being, and cautioned his followers against worshipping him. He wanted them only to follow his teachings. Again, like

Muhammad, Buddha was against all dogma. He wanted people to apply the test of reason and argument to what he said, and not to accept anything just because he had said it. That reminds us of the constant insistence in the Quran, as part of the divine message, on Reason, Knowledge, Thought and Reflection.

To mention another parallel, the principle of Buddhism is more important to the Buddhist faith than the Buddhas who have embodied that principle, just as the message of Islam is more important than the messengers who conveyed it one after the other, until it reached its complete expression in Muhammad, the last and greatest of them all.

To the Buddhists, the Buddha we know, the Prince who renounced his kingdom and found supreme enlightenment under a tree, is not the last manifestation of the Buddha.

Again, the Buddhist teaching about the control of one's mind seems similar to the thought control of the Muslim Sufis.

The missionary spirit, the desire to spread the truth, is common between Buddhism, Islam and Christianity. Buddha wanted his disciples to spread over the earth and take the teaching to all men. Thus there developed, even among the Buddhist laity, a love of travel. The great names of Huen Tsang and Fa Hien come to mind as readily as do those of Ibn Battuta and Marco Polo. An insight into the spread of Buddhism can be gained from the life of men like Atisha, one of the great luminaries of the Buddhist faith who was born at Dacca nearly a thousand years ago. He is said to have travelled on foot to Tibet through the snowy Himalayas and preached Buddhism there. Before he went to Tibet, he had already travelled to Burma, Thailand, Bali and Ceylon. That is the way Buddhism spread over the greater part of the ancient world, including the Indo-Pakistan Sub-continent, where it was later wiped out by physical onslaughts led by men like Sankaracharya.

Incidentally, Udegram, in Swat, was a great seminary of Buddhism. The missionaries, artists and sculptors of Udegram were much in demand in China and Tibet.

One of the outstanding contributions of Buddhism to the cause of human progress is the educational system that evolved through the Buddhist monasteries which spread over a large part of the world and

112

later on influenced the monastic institutions of Christianity. In this Sub-continent, the two greatest educational forces have been Buddhism and Islam before Christianity arrived in the British period. The essence of the Buddhist and Muslim educational movements was to make education available to every human being, and not to let it remain the exclusive privilege of the chosen few. It is interesting to recall that the Buddhists adopted Pali, the language of the common people, as a medium of instruction, just as the Muslims developed the regional dialects of the Sub-continent, such as Bengali and Gujrati, into literary languages.

As we have seen, Islam and Buddhism, notwithstanding their divergent outlook on life, have affinities of a fundamental character. The emphasis on the equality and fraternity of human beings and the right of the human individual to be educated and cared for, are two of the most striking of these affinities. As for the divergences, they exist largely on the religious and philosophical plane, and are natural as between any two systems of thought and belief. They deserve separate treatment, and it is not my purpose to go into them on the present occasion.

Historically, Muslims and Buddhists have had a great deal to do with each other in this Sub-continent. When the Muslims under Muhammad bin Qasim conquered Sind as a measure of reprisals against the depredations of the Sindhi pirates, they were welcomed and helped by the Buddhists against their Hindu rulers. The Muslim success was, to no small extent, due to this particular factor. Muhammad bin Qasim had, at the outset, extended the privileged status of "The People of the Book" to the Hindus and the Buddhists who, by this proclamation, became entitled to the same protection from his Government as the Christians and the Jews. This was particularly reassuring to the Buddhists (the Arab historians call them 'Samanis,' a word which may have some connection with 'Samanera', the Buddhist word for novices) who were unhappy under the Hindu yoke. I am happy to say that I am not aware of any example in history of Buddhist-Muslim relations having ever been disturbed by the kind of tensions that have often developed (sometimes acutely, as under the Guptas in the fourth century of the Christian era) between the Hindus and the Buddhists.

113

In the field of art, we are the privileged custodians of the larger part of Gandhara art, which represents the earliest attempt at making a physical image of the Buddha, an image which is one of the most beautiful representations of the human form in the history of the world's art. Incidentally, the Persian word *but* which is used for an idol, a beautiful person, and a sweetheart is probably derived from 'Budd' which is the usual word in Arabic for the Buddha. It is sometimes said that the Buddhist sculpture of Mathura is contemporary with Gandhara, but the probability, if I may say so, does not lie that way. It s e e m s that the B u d d h a image was first conceived in Gandhara and Buddhist sculpture moved downwards from the north. However that may be, the remains of Gandhara art in Pakistan are one of our proud possessions. Taxila, Takht Bahai, Dir, Swat and a number of other places are lasting monuments of the greatness of Gandhara art. May I recall that part of the ashes of the Buddha himself were buried at the Dharamarajika Stupa at Taxila and were given away as a gift, along with a silver scroll that described them, to Ceylon by the British Government in 1935. I wish our brethren of Ceylon joy in the possession of this sacred relic, but I must confess I feel sorry at having been deprived of the privilege of keeping it.

There are a number of other associations. One of the many lives of the Buddha is said to have been spent at Taxila. It was in this town that there flourished a world-famous Buddhist University, an institution which is frequently mentioned in the Jataka stories, namely, stories of the many lives of the Buddha. Asoka, the great Buddhist Emperor, was Viceroy at Taxila before he ascended the imperial throne, and his son Kunala was Viceroy after him. The northern and north-western parts of Pakistan still have a number of Asoka edicts in stone at various places. Kautilya, the famous author of the *Arthashastra*, is also said to have been born in Taxila. I believe that Buddhism spread into China from Peshawar, the Purushpura of the Buddhist days, where a great gathering of Buddhist scholars and monks took place during the reign of Kanishka. A whole chain of monasteries spread over West Pakistan.

In East Pakistan also we have a wealth of Buddhist art and architecture. We have Buddhist remains in Mahasthangarh, Paharpur and Mainamati dating back to the Mauryia, the Pala and the Chandra dynasties. The monastery at Paharpur is regarded as the biggest

114

Buddhist monastery in the whole of Asia. There were other remains which have either disappeared or have not been traced so far. For example, there are the Chakra Shala monastery and the Pandit Vihara, both at Chittagong, the sites of which are known and await excavation.

It is also a matter of pride for us in Pakistan that we are in possession of the original manuscript of the first life of the Buddha in Pali. The manuscript is being edited by Professor Tucci, the renowned Italian scholar.

In Pakistan the Buddhist community, numbering more than half a million, are among our most welcome and valued citizens. They are believed to be the descendants of the original Buddhists of this Sub-continent, and represent an unbroken tradition. We are happy to think that, if the followers of Dr. Ambedkar who turned to Buddhism primarily with the object of getting away from the Caste System, are excluded, there are more Buddhists in Pakistan than in India. The Pakistan Government has always been anxious to protect and safeguard the interests of the Buddhist community and to promote its welfare. Scholarships were first given for the Buddhists more than 15 years ago. I am glad that the community is doing well and is contributing more and more to the vigour and variety of our national life. Recently, a Buddhist University has been planned in Dacca, and the Government has already granted a sizeable plot of land for it. Let me hope that this University will be established soon. Let me also hope that it will grow and flourish as a centre of Buddhist learning. It has been my dream to see a University of comparative religion and Central Asian studies at Taxila. Let us hope that that University too will be established on that ancient soil, one of the most ancient university campuses in the world.

You have spoken of the need for a Buddhist monastery in Karachi. I wholeheartedly support the proposal. After all, in this great city of ours, if the Muslims have their mosques and the Hindus their temples, if the Christians have their churches and the Parsis their synagogues, why should the Buddhists not have their monastery? I hope you have it soon. It will add another feather to Karachi's cap.

Today we live in an uncertain world, which is changing rapidly around us. Circumstances arise over which we often have no control.

115

We have a great deal to learn from each other, and to forgive each other much. And when we think of the present situation, we must, if we want to go on, turn to the deeper realities of life for inspiration and sustenance. We are cheered on our way by the hopeful message of the Quran. And the last words of the Buddha come to us too, with their message of persistent effort and self-reliance. When the Great One was about to depart this life, his favourite disciple, Ananda, asked him what was going to happen to his followers after him.

"Be a lamp unto thyself," said the Buddha, "Hold fast to truth. Seek no other refuge. Work out thine own salvation." These are great words, some of the greatest ever uttered by man. And if we carried them home with us from this meeting, the meeting would have served its purpose and we would have done something for our own benefit.

BOOKS AS PART OF MUSLIM CULTURE

Speech on the occasion of the Adamjee Prize Distribution at Karachi

When we Muslims speak of books we must remember that books have a special claim on us and we on them. The Prophet brought us a Book, and the first word that came to him from that Book was اقرا "read". Again, the people who are closest to us are those to whom earlier Prophets brought earlier Books. These "People of the Book" are the Christians and the Jews, but Muhammad bin Qasim, the youngest and most amazing general of history who conquered Sind in the eighth century of the Christian era, regarded the Hindus and the Buddhists also as "People of the Book".

The Muslim love of books, which stems from Islam itself, is abundantly reflected in Muslim literature. To take one or two stray examples, the great Almutanabbi thought that the best companion in the world was a book:

$$و خير جليس فى الزّمان كتابٌ$$

The immortal Hafiz of Shiraz longed for a little leisure to enjoy a book in a corner of a garden, far from the maddening crowd :

$$فراغتى و كتابى و گوشهٔ چمنى$$

This is not to speak of Omar Khayyam who regarded "A Book of Verses underneath the Bough" as an indispensable ingredient of happiness.

It is a matter of great privilege for us to be present here this evening when the President is honouring the Adamjee Prize by giving it to its distinguished recipients, the four brilliant authors of our two national languages—Urdu and Bengali—who have produced works of outstanding merit. This prize, which is administered by the Pakistan Writers' Guild, has already done great service to our national literature by promoting creative effort in the field of poetry, drama and fiction. The importance of creative literature can hardly be over-emphasized. It is an asset of lasting value, a joy for ever. It presents the soul of a people to the rest of the world, the spirit of an age to future ages. And it enriches the heritage of the human race. In a very real sense of the word, Shakespeare is among the most valuable possessions of the British people, Goethe of the Germans, Hafiz of Iran and Iqbal of Pakistan. And yet they belong to all men, for the great ones among mankind belong to all mankind.

The Dawood Prize, which is also administered by the Writers' Guild, and with which, in spite of my not being a member of the Guild, I have the honour to be associated as Chairman of the Panel of Judges, is designed to promote and accord recognition to research on our cultural heritage and the freedom movement. This is of vital importance for a proper understanding of the historical forces that led to the creation of Pakistan, and of the way in which Partition and the transfer of power became inevitable. The study of the past is important as the future has to be built upon it.

The Adamjee Prize and the Dawood Prize, for which we must all be thankful to the Houses of Adamjee and Dawood, have already gone a long way to encourage creative and research literature, but I wish to submit that we have a much longer way to go and a much wider area to cover. The virile character of our people and their rising aspirations for a better life cannot rest content with only one or two aspects of creative or research writing. We already have a rich past in creative and research literature which is being enriched further by the contribution of contemporary writers and scholars. But literature, like life itself, must be multi-dimensional. We still suffer from serious shortcomings in important spheres of writing. We have no standard works in our national languages on science, economics, engineering, medicine, military science and, if you will pardon a reference to my own favourite subject, banking. I need hardly refer to history or philosophy, in which the deficiencies of our national languages are already known and felt. At present we have to approach all these subjects through English and other European languages, but if our national languages have to become a proper medium of communication and instruction, we have to produce a literature on these important subjects in Bengali and Urdu without delay so as to familiarize the younger generation with them through our national media. Only then shall we be able to advance the study of scientific and technical subjects on a nation wide basis as we must do if we are to call ourselves Muslims. The spirit of enquiry and the pursuit of knowledge is a part of the fundamental structure of Islamic culture. The Quran repeatedly exhorts us to علم Knowledge, عقل reason, شعور understanding and فكر thought. Again and again, it draws our attention to the events of history and the phenomena of Nature, and asks us to think

120

زمردان پرطاوس روسی دیبا / کفارش تیغ زن صدهزار

دکرشته زیر شمشیر و تیر / زکشتن بود فتنه را ناگزیر

Sikandar Nama—illustrated—Transcribed by Saifuddin Qadri in 1831 A.D. (Peshawar Museum).

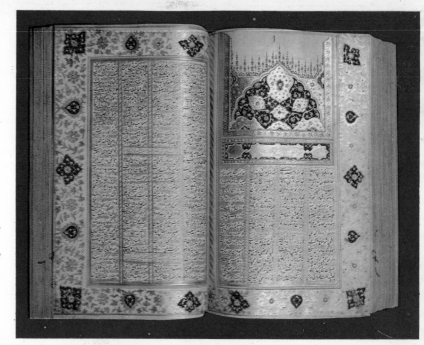

An illuminated page from the 'Shahnameh' of Firdausi. Early 18th century A. D. (National Museum, Karachi).

A page from 'Baaz Nama', a book on Falconry. Late 18th century A. D. (National Museum, Karachi)

Specimen of Nastaliq signed by the Calligrapher Imam Wirdi. The border is decorated with floral design. (National Museum Karachi)

A specimen of 'tughra' in the form of parrot. Mughul School, 18th century A. D. (Lahore Museum).

upon the creation of the Heaven and the Earth and to know that it is not in vain:

يتفكرون في خلق السموات والارض ٠ ربنا ماخلقت هذا باطلاه [1]

The Prophet set the highest value on the pursuit of knowledge:

اطلب العلم من المهد الى اللحد

"Seek ye knowledge from the cradle to the grave," said he. Again:

طلب العلم فريضة على مسلم ومسلمة

The pursuit of knowledge is a duty for every Muslim man and woman.

The place that the pursuit of knowledge occupies in the Muslim scheme of things is probably best illustrated in a verse attributed to Ali Ibn Abu Talib:

لا فخر الا لاهل العلم انهم
على الهدى لمن استهدى ادلاء

There is no pride except for the men of learning, for verily It is they who are on the right path and guide others to that path.

The study of science and the application of the scientific method to the phenomena of life is the real source of power in the modern age. And when we speak of science, we have to remember that it owes its existence to the Muslims. As Briffault said, "Science is the most momentous contribution of Muslim civilization to the modern world." The world has seldom produced men of the stature of Ibn Sina, Ibn Rushd, Ibn-ul-Haitham, Ibn Khaldun, Yaqut Hamavi, Jabir bin Hayyan, Zakariyya Razi, Ibn Baitar and Alberuni. Even a man like Omar Khayyam, whose fame now rests, by an irony of chance, on his quatrains only, was one of the greatest mathematicians of all time. It may be of interest to mention that among other things, he was the author of a calendar which is more accurate than the Gregorian Calendar. These are only a few of the great names that come to mind. The story of the rise and fall

---

1. The Quran, Vol I, III. 191

of Muslim civilization is the story of the ebb and flow of the spirit of enquiry among the Muslims. The rise of Europe and America and the pre-dominant position they have occupied in the last few centuries is accounted for mainly by science and technology. We have to recapture our scientific tradition and make science and technology our own once again if we are to hold our head high and occupy a place of honour among the nations.

As regards economics, there has to be greater interest in the subject and a large number of good books on it in our national languages if we are to have a proper grip on the problems of daily life. This is all the more important as Pakistan is now humming with economic activity all round. As for engineering, medicine, banking and military science there are hardly any books worth the name in Bengali or Urdu. They have yet to be written. And may I say that translations, however good, are a poor substitute for original work. We have distinguished scientists, economists, engineers, doctors and other technologists. Why should they not produce original works in their own subjects in our national languages?

I am sorry to have bothered you with this recital of our difficulties and deficiencies in the matter of books. I feel that the time has come when the patronage of Government and of the President himself, who has done so much to encourage books and authors in this country, should be extended to the fields of science, economics and other important subjects like medicine, engineering, military science and banking, which have a direct contribution to make to the progress and welfare of our people. It is necessary to have prizes and fellowships instituted to encourage the study of these scientific and technological subjects and the writing of good books on them in our national languages. Let us hope that the excellent example set by the Houses of Adamjee and Dawood will be followed by those who, by the grace of God, have the means and the will to help this great and noble cause.

OUR CLASSICS

The classics of a language are vital to its progress and development. They are a fountain-head of inspiration, whether we follow their tradition or rebel against it. They may attract or they may repel, but they are a standard of reference all the same. Neglect of the classics means literary anarchy.

The classics of every language have their importance, but the most important are those of the language or languages which have preserved for posterity the basic tradition of a culture or civilization. For example, Greek and Latin are important for Europe, and Arabic and Persian for the Muslims of the Indo-Pakistan Sub-continent. European culture has a Graeco-Roman foundation and the languages of Europe turn to the Greek and Roman classics for their models. Similarly, Indo-Muslim culture, which has held sway over this Sub-continent for more than a thousand years, is based on Arabic and Persian. It is as difficult to master Urdu without knowing Arabic and Persian as it is to have a proper appreciation of English without a knowledge of Greek and Latin.

Arabic arrived in this Sub-continent with traders and invaders from Arabia. Both in East and West Pakistan, the Arab connection is older than Islam. After the Arab occupation of Sind, a great literary tradition was established in this Sub-continent. It was a tradition which, before long, produced a poet of the status of Abul-ala-as-Sindi, who finds a place in the *Hamasah* of Abu Tammam, the best known anthology of Arabic poetry apart from the *Sabaa Muallaqah*. At a later stage, we have a lexicographer of the eminence of Imam Saghani of Lahore and a scholar of the stature of Mulla Abdul Hakim of Sialkot. Even in more recent times, we have had the writings of Shah Waliullah of Delhi, Mir Ghulam Ali Azad of Bilgram, Maulana Fazle Haq of Khairabad and Nawab Siddiq Hasan of Bhopal. Even the late Inayatullah Mashriqi, who wrote his *Tadhkira* about forty years ago, added to it an introduction, of more than 144 pages, in Arabic. In our own day, the Arabic tradition is represented with unique distinction by Maulana Abdul Aziz Memon who, as a scholar in Arabic literature, has hardly any compeer in the world today.

The Arab conquest did not last. Hardly a century and a half had passed when Arab influence began to wane and India lost the opportunity of having direct contact with the Arabs. This was a development of far reaching significance and affected the whole level of Muslim culture in the Sub-continent. The Turks, Afghans and Mughals, who came after the Arabs, used Persian as their court language. The political influence of Iran in West Pakistan dates back to the Acheamenian period, about 600 B.C., when the province known to archaeologists as Gandhara was a part of the Achaemenian Empire with a satrap exercising viceregal authority from Taxila. The Persian language, however, was not established as a cultural institution in the Sub-continent till the days of Mahmud of Ghazna. Since then, it has been the predominant influence in Indo-Muslim culture. It has produced poets of the stature of Masud Sa'd Salman, Amir Khusru, Ghalib, Bedil, Nasir Ali, Ghani Kashmiri, Shibli, Girami and Iqbal. The contribution to Persian prose made by the Indo-Pakistan Sub-continent is no less important and we have a large number of literary and scientific works of high excellence. The first existing *Tadhkira*, or biographical anthology of Persian poets, namely *Lubab al-Albab*, was compiled by Aufi in Uchh in West Pakistan in the 7th century A.H. An even earlier *Tadhkira* which is known to be the earliest ever written but which has been lost to us, was also produced in Multan, in West Pakistan. The first *Tadhkira* of women poets of Persian, the *Jawahir al-Ajaib*, was written in Sind by Fakhri Haravi in the 10th century A.H. Even *Tadhkiras* of Urdu poets are, upto the 13th century A.H., mostly in Persian, including those written by famous Urdu poets like Mir Taqi, Mushafi and Shefta.

As regards lexicography, with the exception of the first three dictionaries of Persian which were produced in Iran, the important lexicons of the Persian language were compiled in the Sub-continent up to the 13th century A.H. Historical writing began in Pakistan with the *Chach Nameh* and the *Tabaqat-i-Nasiri* in the 7th century A.H. and we have had since then a number of historians of great distinction like Ziauddin Burney, Afif, Ahmad Thattavi, Khawaja Nizamuddin, Abdul Qadir Badayuni, Abul Fazl, Abul Qasim Ferishta and Ghulam Husain Tabatabai. All of them wrote in Persian. It may be of interest to recall that Tabatabai wrote his *Siyar al-Mutaakhkhirin* in the British period as late as the nineteenth century. Even in the beginning of the twentieth century, Khudadad Khan wrote his *History of Sind* in Persian.

Anquetil Duperron, a French scholar who travelled in India

in the eighteenth century, made an interesting observation in regard to the use of Persian in the country at the time. Writing about the languages in use in India, he says that Sanskrit was an important language of the country but it was a dead language. The language more useful and understood almost everywhere in the country "until my return in 1762" was Persian. This language was current even in the Maldip Island in the east of India.[1]

Lest there be any misapprehension on the subject, I ought to make it clear that the influence of Arabic and Persian in East Pakistan has been at least as great as in West Pakistan. The study of Arabic has always had a prominent place in the educational system of Bengal and even today there are more Arabic Madrassahs in East than in West Pakistan. In the British days, the Muslims of Bengal and Assam successfully sponsored a scheme for the maintenance of Arabic studies as a major part of the curriculum in the Lower and Higher Secondary stages in the face of the growing influence of English. The vocabulary of the Bengali language contains a generous admixture of Arabic words, and I am informed that in Chittagonian Bengali, the Arabic element is as high as 25 per cent.

Persian has been an even greater influence, and the name of Bengal occupies a prominent place in some of the classics of the Persian language. Sultan Ghiathuddin, one of the great kings of Bengal, is said to have invited Hafiz to his kingdom. Hafiz could not come, but gave proof of his gratitude to the Sultan for his invitation by immortalising him and the kingdom of Bengalah in one of his famous odes:

خامش مشو که کار تو از ناله می رود   حافظ ز شوق مجلس سلطان غیاث دین

O Hafiz, let not thy longing for the court of Sultan Ghiathuddin
Make thee silent, for thy affairs will be furthered by thy lamentation.

زین قند پارسی که به بنگاله می رود   شکر شکن شوند همه طوطیان هند

The songsters of the land of Ind shall relish
This sweet Persian that goes to Bangalah.

---

1. Iftikhar Husain, *Anquetil Duperrom—18th Century French Scholar and Traveller*, (unpublished)

Hafiz was not alone. There were many among the literary celebrities of Iran, who were attracted to India by the magnificent patronage of Muslim kings, but who, for one reason or another, could not come to the land that held such promise for them.

Saib of Ispahan once sent the following couplet to Jafar Khan, one of the premier nobles of Aurangzeb's court, who rewarded him liberally for it :

دور دستان را به احسان یاد کردن همت است ٭ ور نه هر نخلی به پای خود ثمر می افگند

'Tis generous to think of the hands that are far away;
Else, every tree doth cast its fruit at its own feet.

Among the fortunate few, who came and made India their second home, the names of Iraqi of Hamadan, Kalim of Kashan, Urfi of Shiraz, Naziri of Nishapur and Ali Hazin of Lahij come to mind.

Inscriptions on mosques and tombs in East Pakistan occur both in Arabic and Persian till the Mughal period but are confined to Persian in Mughal times. Persian flourished in Bengal under the Mughal Empire and continued to do so even later. The history of Bengal entitled *Riyaz al-Salatin* was written by Ghulam Husain Salim in Persian in the eighteenth century. Hamidullah wrote his *Tarikh-i-Islamabad*, a history of Chittagong, in Persian in the latter half of the nineteenth century. A very interesting comment is made on the influence of Arabic and Persian in East Pakistan by Abdul Ali of Chittagong, who wrote his *Sahifat-al-Amal-wa-Mirat-al-Ahwal*, about eighty years ago. According to him, although the use of the Persian language had become rare at the time his book was written, it was current like a mother tongue thirty years earlier :

زبان فارسی اگرچه درین دیار اسلام آباد به صفت عنقائی موصوف گردیده اما به اعتبار سابق الحال یعنی قبل سی سال زمانی بود که هم چون زبان مادری مروج براوج کمال

He goes on to say that of the languages he knew, namely, Persian, Arabic, Urdu, Bengali and English, he prefers Arabic and Persian. But as, in Bengal, Persian comes before Arabic in the curriculum, he has written his book in the Persian language :

128

از لغات مختلفہ معلومہ ام کہ فارسی و عربی وارد و و بنگالی و انگریزی است ۔ لغت فارسی و عربی را نیکو تر دانم لیکن در اینجا زبان فارسی قبل عربی می خوانند ۔ از ایں جا کتاب ہذا بہ لغت فارسی قلمی شد

Thereafter, Abdul Ali addresses a touching exhortation to his son, urging him to take up the study of Persian in case he himself does not live long enough to educate him. He wishes his son to read all his writings and to imbibe wisdom from them. That is his last will and testament :

اے ریحان باغ زندگی اگر من پیش تربیت تو درخت ہستی بہ بندم وصیت من بتو ایں است کہ بہ فارسی دانی مصنف طبع رجوع آوردہ از مضامین مصنفہ ام نیکو واقف شدہ بہر ہمہ گوشش ہوشش بر نگاری

The Persian language influenced not only Urdu and Bengali, but a large number of local languages in the Sub-continent as well. As far as Urdu is concerned, while its foundation lies in Sanskrit or one or the other of Sanskrit dialects, its super-structure is almost entirely Persian. Even Arabic words have come to Urdu mostly through the medium of the Persian language. I understand that the same is generally true of Bengali. It need hardly be added that the same Muslim kings of Bengal who used Persian in their official correspondence patronised and promoted Bengali as a literary language.

It may be of some interest to mention that, in the famous *Dars-i-Nizami* of Farangi Mahal, the prescribed Arabic text books usually had a Persian commentary in the margin. Persian had been the court language of the greater part of the Sub-continent upto 1837 A.D., when the British rulers replaced it with English. It did continue, however, to be the language of the Mughal Court, such as it was, up to 1857, when the last semblance of Muslim power in the Sub-continent was blown away like smoke[1]. Persian still continued to be the language of culture and private correspondence till the turn of the century but the influence of English had become predominant by that time. Indeed, but for the work of Shibli and Iqbal, we might have seen the last of Persian language and literature in the Sub-continent by now.

This is the brief story of Arabic and Persian I have to tell. These two languages shaped the culture of the Indo-Pakistan Sub-continent

---

1. Persian remained the official language in Hyderabad Deccan till 1885.

for centuries and maintained their dominion over the minds of men through the ebb and flow of history. Just as, in medieval Europe, Latin was the favourite language of the clergy and French of the aristocracy, Arabic in this Sub-continent has been associated generally with Islamic studies, and Persian with administrative and cultural activity. So far as Urdu is concerned, I am quite certain that its future progress depends on our getting nearer to Arabic and Persian rather than in getting away from them. I venture to suggest that the same is true of Bengali. Apart from the religious significance that Arabic has for the Muslims, it is the custodian of the best and noblest traditions of science and the humanities. As far as Persian is concerned, if we were to go back a hundred years, we would find it a common medium of a common Muslim culture in the whole of the Indo-Pakistan Sub-continent. The nearer we get to the Persian language, therefore, the nearer we get to our cultural heritage and the nearer we get to each other. I would, for this if for no other reason, like to make a plea for greater attention to Arabic and Persian in Pakistan.

A word about Sanskrit. As I have already said, Sanskrit (or one or the other of its dialects) is the foundation of Urdu, which derives its verbs, prepositions and conjunctions largely from Sanskrit. The same, if I may say so, is the case with Bengali. Yet there is such a dearth of Sanskrit scholarship in this country that it is time for us to sit up and take notice. I would very much like to see Chairs of Sanskrit installed in more than one University in Pakistan and I suggest that, if the Pakistan Writers' Guild agrees with me, it may take up this matter with the authorities concerned. Only by promoting the study of Arabic, Persian and Sanskrit can Urdu and Bengali literature attain that level of excellence that we desire. Lest you accuse me of inflicting too many classical languages on you, may I remind you of the great Alberuni. May I remind you also of British scholars like Sir William Jones and Professor E.B. Cowell, who knew all the three languages—Arabic, Persian and Sanskrit. Surely, it is not too much to expect that some of us will study one or more of these languages, if not all three, and make our contribution to the preservation and continuance of the great traditions of our culture.

130

INCENTIVES TO WRITERS

Speech at the Annual Function of the Pakistan Writers' Guild at Karachi, 1964

When we speak of incentives to writers we must remember the variety of writers we have to deal with. There are writers and writers. Some write for a living, others for pleasure. Some write because they must, being moved by inspiration and swayed by the inner compulsion of genius. And inspiration comes when it wishes and where it wishes; it is not at the beck and call of human beings. When it comes to a man like Shelley, it finds expression without effort, as the wind makes music in the reeds. There are others, including some of the greater ones, whose genius consists, in the words of Carlyle, in an infinite capacity for taking pains, who, like Tennyson, have to struggle with themselves before they are able to say what they want to say.

But, in spite of this diversity among writers, there are certain things that are common among them. To start with, all writers, great or small, can do with good health and a reasonable amount of comfort in life. It may or may not be true to say that great writers are helped to their masterpieces by disappointment in love or by social upheavals around them; but it is certainly no more than a romantic untruth to say that poverty, ill health or the prospect of early death are an aid to great writing. It did no harm to Goethe to live in health and comfort and live to be eighty three, nor did it hurt Shakespeare to have a modest income. If Mir Taqi had not been quite so penniless, he would not have ceased to be a poet. The early deaths of men like Keats and Chatterton or Miraji and Majaz are, to say the least, regrettable. They could have written more and possibly better if they had been healthier and had lived longer. A society which wants to get the best out of its writers need not kill them prematurely. Indeed, it must look after them, and make it easy for them to do their writing.

The greatest satisfaction of an artist is to express himself, to be able to say what he wishes to say. But self-expression cannot bring satisfaction unless it takes the form of communication with other human beings. A speaker without an audience or a writer without a reading public is like a voice in the wilderness, a cry in the night. We have to provide facilities for the writer to write and the reader to read. This means, in the first place, that there should be more educated people in the country. No country can hope to make any real progress without education. Pakistan has educational plans and they are going ahead but we have to remind ourselves that without active effort on the part of each one of us, and the determination to conquer mass ignorance, these plans may take longer to mature than we can afford. Education delayed is education denied, and with the rapid growth of population in the country the longer we take to spread the light of knowledge among our people, the greater is the likelihood of our living in perpetual ignorance as a nation.

In order to promote education we need an abundance of reading material and good libraries. At present libraries are too few and books too costly and too scarce; we need more books and cheaper books. The printing industry needs help and guidance to bring printing costs down and place books within the reach of every educated person.

With an educated reading public the writer, be he a genius or a mediocrity, will be encouraged to do his best. But he will need some more concrete assistance if he is to continue as a writer and fulfil his mission. Writing materials and printing facilities have to be cheaper and more plentiful. We have had the strange experience of shortage of paper even in East Pakistan, where our biggest paper mills are located. We trust that there will be no recurrence of such a state of affairs in future.

There should be recognition for good books. The British regime used to encourage deserving writers in this Sub-continent by giving them honours and awards and cash prizes. The munificence of Muslim Kings, particularly the Mughals, to poets and writers has been proverbial. In the earlier years of Pakistan there was hardly any appreciation shown of this important aspect of national activity. In the last few years, however, there has been a welcome change in attitude. The Government has turned its attention in real earnest to this matter. The Houses of Adamjee and Dawood have instituted literary prizes. Much more has, however, to be done in this direction and I appeal to the richer ones of this country to come forward and follow the example set by Adamjee and Dawood.

More than anything else, the writer has to be accorded social recognition as a writer, to be cared for and looked after as such, and to be respected as such. Do not let us underrate the importance of the writer. He is more conscious of the significance of life than we are, more deeply aware of the universe around us, and more in communion with the myriad manifestations of beauty that often pass us by. He seeks to bring human beings closer to each other and seeks to make them look upon each other more kindly through a greater understanding of the joys and sorrows that are common to all of us. Do not let us underrate him. Do we not know how the work of Turgenev served to hasten the abolition of serfdom in Russia; how Charles Dickens in England and Emile Zola in France drew pointed attention to the social evils of their time and paved the way for social reform; how Mazzini became the mouthpiece of the Italian risorgimento and how in our own day the work of Iqbal has become the foundation stone of a new state, this Pakistan of ours which we hold so dear.

We have so far regarded the writer as a mere adjunct to society; we forget that he is very much a member of it and has a right to live as a writer. As long as we consider him a superfluity to be tolerated, benevolently or otherwise, and not an asset to society to be thankful for, he will find it difficult to live among us and call himself a writer. Unless we give him honour, prestige, status, privileges and facilities such as we give to our politicians, civil servants, doctors, engineers and bankers, we shall not get the full value out of him. He will continue to be infectiously melancholy as he often is today and vaguely rebellious against nothing in particular. We should change, and let him change as well. Only by respecting the writer and letting him respect himself shall we be able to say to ourselves that we have done something for him. Thus, and only thus, can we serve the cause of writing and the writer and have the satisfaction of feeling that there will always be in this country great writers and great literature.

FINE ARTS AND ECONOMIC DEVELOPMENT

Speech at the Bulbul Academy of Fine Arts at Dacca, 1963

Pakistan is an underdeveloped country engaged in a vast development effort. The object is to raise the standard of living of our people, to combat poverty, ignorance and disease and to give every man, woman and child a better deal in life.

These are not catch phrases. The task of economic development is the biggest we have before us today. Unless we tackle that task in real earnest and with some chance of success, the political freedom we have won, after such a hard struggle, will have no meaning.

Political freedom is not an end in itself; it is only a means to an end. And what is that end? It is that we give our people freedom from hunger and want, and deliver them from the squalor in which they have lived for ages. That again is not an end in itself, but only a means to another end. And what is that other end?

It is that our people, having achieved freedom from want and worry, should be able to turn their minds to the higher values of life, that we as a people should be able to live more fully, more happily and in greater conformity with the ideals we love and cherish.

It is then, and only then, that we shall be able to make our contribution to world thought and world culture; only then that we shall join and, may be, some day lead the onward march of humanity.

For the present, we have the plans and programmes of development on our hands. Economic development has been the preoccupation of the leaders of the Pakistan movement from the very beginning. The budget presented by the late Mr. Liaquat Ali Khan as the last Finance Minister of the late Government of India emphasized the need of the development of the Indus Basin and the Ganges-Brahmaputra basin—in other words, East and West Pakistan.

The lack of economic opportunity among the people of the Pakistan areas was recognised by the more fair-minded outsiders, like Professor Coupland, as one of the main causes of the demand for the partition of India.

Pakistan was fought for and won because we wanted to live our lives in our own way, to preserve our culture and to build up our economic life. It is hardly possible to think of preservation of culture without economic progress, nor would economic progress have much meaning if it could not help in protecting culture.

139

We are just now in the thick of our economic effort. The first Five Year Plan, the total size of which, in financial terms, was Rs. 1,080 crore, came to an end on the 30th June 1960. On the 1st of July 1960 began the Second Five Year Plan with an estimated cost of Rs. 1,900 crore which subsequently had to be increased to Rs. 2,300 crores. We are halfway through the Second Plan. The Third Plan is going to be much bigger than the Second, and future Plans are going to be bigger and bigger still.

With the help of all these Plans we hope to reach a stage when Pakistan can itself generate the resources needed for its development and not have to depend on outside assistance for its economic programmes. The economists are fond of calling this the "take off" stage. If all goes well, we expect to reach that stage in twenty years or so from now.

That shows how big the development effort has to be and how long it is likely to take us to reach the "take-off" stage, which the advanced countries of the world reached a long time ago. It is now time to ask ourselves the question: In what way is economic development related to cultural activity, particularly to the fine arts? The answer is two-fold.

In the first place, the development of the fine arts is a part of economic development. No economic effort can be fruitful without universal education in the country, and a great part of the driving force for economic and educational effort comes from the fine arts. A stirring piece of poetry, a beautiful picture or a sublime specimen of architecture, can fill the soul with inspiration, and raise in us the power to change the world around us. The first two plans of Pakistan have not given adequate attention to this important aspect of our lives but it is bound to claim greater importance in future planning.

Secondly, in order that our fine arts should inspire us to greater and more creative effort, it is necessary that we have the right type of fine arts. It is not every kind of poetry which bids us to be up and doing. Indeed, there is a great deal of poetry which, if we let it take hold of us, could easily lead us to suicide. There are paintings which open our eyes to the beauty around us; there are others which merely confuse and depress us when we look at them. There is music which makes us march forward, there is also music which puts us to sleep. There is architecture which uplifts the mind and soul of man, there is also architecture which is vulgar, unedifying, degrading. What then is the kind of poetry and painting, music and architecture that we want? We in Pakistan have to make our choice.

The more advanced countries of the world can perhaps afford to promote the kind of fine arts which thrive on a negation of life and activity, but can we afford to do so? Would we be wise, for instance, if we were to encourage existentialist poetry, the poetry that strips life of all significance?

Of course, we cannot dictate to the artist. There is no means of making him produce things to order. If his soul is full of disappointment and despair, his art is bound to be full of it as well. But it is a question whether we, as a people, should patronise and promote such art. I beg to suggest that we give our most careful thought to this matter. If we are to achieve the great objective we have set before ourselves, if we are to rescue our people from poverty, ignorance and disease, should we not give our patronage and support to the artist who inspires us to high endeavour and brings us the message of hope for the future? And should we not discourage the one who does not?

If this is what we should do, we ought to take a good look at every piece of poetry, painting or music, at every expression of the artistic impulse, and see whether it is the right type of art for us. I am not asking the Government to intervene—far from it—but I am asking that every one of us, as a thinking individual, should face the problem fairly and squarely, come to a clear conclusion, and act accordingly.

Speaking for myself, may I suggest that there is a wealth of inspiration in our folk songs and folk dances which is not yet fully known. These songs and dances are full of the spontaneous joy of life, a joy which most of the so-called classical compositions lack. Folk traditions in art are like the phenomena of nature. They have grown like grass in the field or trees in the forest. Classical art is full of sophistication and sophistication kills activity. On the other hand, it is activity we want, creative, persistent activity. We have to build the pattern of our fine arts on the foundations of an active life.

And if we succeed in doing so we shall not only advance the cause of art, but also forge a stronger link between art and life than we can do by any other means.

The world needs something fresh and new, and not merely a repetition of what it has had for hundreds of years. It needs the art that lives and gives life, not the art that is dead or dying and has nothing to give but death and decay. And we in Pakistan need plenty of inspiration to life and activity if we are to tackle the tasks that lie ahead. We are a living people and need the living art, not the art which is the sepulchre of human ideals and human endeavour.

LITERATURE AND SCIENCE

Address to the 8th Anniversary of the Writers' Guild at Karachi, January 1967

There was a school master, they say, somewhere in Pakistan (or to be more precise, in West Pakistan) who taught Arabic in his school. One of his pupils, who was particularly good in class, decided, for some reason which the school master could not understand, to give up Arabic and take up Science instead. Thereupon the school master lost his temper and the story goes that, while the fit was on, he made observations casting serious doubt on the virtue of the boy's female relatives.

Whether the story is true or not, it serves to illustrate the kind of contradiction that exists in the minds of many people between Science and Literature. It may be that in this case the ire of the school master was aroused particularly because Arabic is the language of the Quran and, for us Muslims therefore, a sacred language. Presumably neither master nor pupil were aware of the richness of the Arabic language in scientific terminology and literature. But all this does not affect the main point at issue, nor does our school master by any chance represent an isolated phenomenon.

Are Science and Literature really incompatible with each other? Let us look at them a little closely.

Science, as we all know, is that body of systematised knowledge which relates to one or more aspects of life or the universe and depends for its existence on facts discovered or ascertained through observation or experiment which are capable of standardisation. The interpretation of a body of known facts is called a Theory, and when an invariable and inevitable relationship is established between two facts or sets of facts, we have a Law. If, however, a single fact comes into conflict with, or cannot fit into, a Theory or a Law, it is the Theory or the Law that has to go. The fact cannot be altered or ignored.

Science, thus, is basically knowledge of facts gained through experience. Literature is a wide term but we are using it here in the sense of creative writing, that is, writing including poetry, drama, the novel, the short story, the essay and the epigram, all of which depend on the presentation of ideas, feelings and sensations through the most effective use of language.

Science is primarily an analytical study of a particular aspect of experience. Literature in its higher reaches is, on the other hand, a vision of the basic unity and universality of all experience. It is an attempt at a

145

synthetic view of life, an endeavour to understand life as a totality. As Shelley said:

> I am the eye with which the Universe
> Sees itself and knows itself divine.

It is true that in our own day, Science too is in quest of a basic principle of unity in the Universe, but its approach continues to be based on empirical observation and analysis.

Science is unemotional and depends on objective observation and experiment. Indeed, the 'observer' is often no more than a recording instrument or a machine. Literature on the other hand is subjective, and derives its strength from the emotional response it evokes. Science is of the head, Literature of the heart.

Literature lives in a world where things are known and admired for their individual qualities. Science reduces qualitative differences to differences of quantity.

The literary impulse involves—or so it seems to the artist—creativity in the highest sense of the word. The poet or the writer feels that he is creating something out of nothing; that, in the words of Shakespeare, "as imagination bodies forth the forms of things unknown, his pen gives to airy nothing a local habitation and a name". It may be said on the other hand that science, with all the inspiration that moves the scientist, does not create anything out of nothing—in any case the scientist does not claim that it does; it only discovers and discloses for us what was already there. It is essentially a progressive discovery of facts, and the hidden connections between them, which existed all the time, but were not known before. It could even be said, though not without a touch of exaggeration, that while the literary fraternity can claim to be colleagues and collaborators of God, the scientist is only an examiner and a reporter—the one being engaged in creation, the other in espionage. Such an observation, of course, is hardly fair to the quality of greatness in the spirit of enquiry that moves the scientist, but it nevertheless expresses a distinction well worth noting. Science is the pursuit of Truth, Literature of Beauty and Goodness. Truth cannot be created or improved upon; it can only be ascertained and made known. Beauty is created both by God and man, and Goodness comes from God to man.

146

Literary creation is an act of individual inspiration which cannot be passed on to others. The so-called 'literary schools' are very often poor imitations of the work of great masters, and generally die without leaving any heirs or successors.

As a rule, these schools flourish in isolation. Science, too, is essentially individual inspiration, but scientific work can be and is now generally organised on a collective and cumulative basis. Scientific research is carried on in big institutes and laboratories; it is controlled and directed to certain specific channels of enquiry; and the results are built up over the years. The literary impulse is unpredictable and cannot be commanded at will. As Arnold has put it:-

We cannot kindle when we will
The fire that in the heart resides;
The spirit bloweth and is still,
In mystery our soul abides.

Does Science injure or destroy literary capacity? Can scientific discipline co-exist with the ability to produce work of literary merit? I think the answer to this question is to be found in the life and work of men like Goethe, Leonardo Da Vinci, Bacon, Avicenna, Alberuni and Omar Khayyam. Each of these men was a scientist and an artist at the same time. Goethe, whose work on plants and animals is well known and who, among other things, challenged Newton's Theory of Colours, is one of the greatest poets and play-wrights that the world has known. In the words of Muhammad Iqbal, Pakistan's immortal poet-philosopher and an admirer of Goethe, *Faust* represents the highest level of artistic achievement possible to man. Iqbal hails Goethe as a man who 'though not a prophet, has brought a book,' the book, of course, being *Faust*. Leonardo Da Vinci, who is one of the greatest painters of Europe, was equally interested in scientific experiment. He was a keen student of physics, engineering and human anatomy and was the first man in Europe to have experimented with flight. This was a great distinction, even though a Muslim, Ibn Firnas, had preceded him in the attempt. Bacon not only rationalised the scientific method in his *Novum Organum* but was also a great enough writer to be confused by later generations with Shakespeare. Avicenna, physician and philosopher, the great author of the *Canon* and the *Shifa* and a number of other well known works which have influenced Asia and the Western world for centuries, is also a poet and writer. Alberuni, mathematician, astronomer, historian, and geographer, whose study of Sanskrit and his researches into the religion, mythology, customs and culture of the Hindus entitle him to be regarded as the first Indologist of the world, is also an outstanding man of letters. As regards Omar Khayyam, his Rubaiyat (quatrains) are too well known to need mention, but he was far greater as a mathematician and astronomer than as a poet. His work on equations was an original contribution and the calendar he devised was one of his most outstanding achievements. He is now recognised as one of the greatest mathematicians of all time.

Having regard to the achievements of these outstanding men, can we at all maintain that a scientific bent of mind cannot exist side by side with a literary bent? Even though Science and Literature differ a great deal in their appeal and their purpose, it seems that scientific and literary achievement both have a common source at the higher reaches of life in the creative impulse of man. Man has his moments of vision, of inspiration, of insight. The fall of an apple in a Cambridge garden gave Newton a vision of the Law of Gravitation as in a flash, just as, for Archimedes, the First Law of Hydrostatics emerged suddenly from bath-water, or as the boiling kettle spoke to James Watt, as it were, of the power of steam. This would not seem to be inherently different from the kind of inspiration that came to Keats from the nightingale in his garden or to Shelley from the skylark in the heavens. Some of the mathematical discoveries of the great Gauss appear to a layman to be in the nature of revelation; they are masterpieces of intuition and inspiration. It is said that when a problem of higher mathematics was put to him, he gave the answer immediately, but when he was asked for the process, he wanted a week to work it out. The philosophers, too, have their moments of vision, even when it is the wrong type of vision. Nietzsche tells us, for example, how the idea of Eternal Recurrence came to him all of a sudden in a deep moonlit night.

It could be said, with truth, that literary and scientific activity may not manifest itself in the same man at the same moment. The literary impulse and the scientific impulse may succeed each other in point of time. This, however, does not in any way affect the possibility of their peaceful and, may we add, useful co-existence as part of the

148

same personality.

I have spoken just now about some of the greatest minds in the history of the human race. Let us also take a look at the second line of genius. Robert Bridges, Arthur Canon Doyle, Somerset Maugham, Said Naficey and Hakim Momin Khan were all physicians by profession, and each one achieved lasting fame in literature. Robert Bridges is one of the famous poets of the English language. He was Poet Laureate for seventeen years in the early part of this century. Speaking of Canon Doyle, detective fiction is generally full of scientific terminology and techniques. Had not Sherlock Holmes been a scientific observer trained in the inductive way of thinking, he could not have performed the miracles he is called upon to undertake. Somerset Maugham is one of the popular novelists of the English language in our time. Said Naficey is one of the great literary figures of Iran in the twentieth century, and Momin Khan is one of the most outstanding poets of the Urdu language. Lewis Carrol (or the Reverend Charles Lutwidge Dodgson, to give him his real name) was a mathematician who wrote those immortal household classics, *Alice in Wonderland* and *Alice In The Looking Glass*. William James, an outstanding psychologist and philosopher, was an equally outstanding writer of the English language, probably greater than his brother Henry. Arthur Eddington, one of the keenest minds in modern physics, and author of *The Nature Of The Physical World* and *Science And The Unseen World* has a refinement and maturity of style which is rare even among those whose fame rests chiefly on literary writing. Julian Huxley, one of the foremost biologists of our time, is well known as a lucid and attractive writer. Bertrand Russell, a mathematician and a philosopher, is one of the best known literary figures of the twentieth century and has received the Nobel Prize for literature.

We also have men like H.G. Wells and Jules Verne who, though primarily writers, have produced what has come to be known as scientific fiction. That is a name for fancies and phantasies which appear to be impossible inventions of the human imagination to start with, but become common experience in course of time. These imaginings are a by-product of man's primeval struggle against Nature. Man seeks to control his environment to his own advantage, but can do so only partially and gradually, and where he finds himself powerless to do anything, at any rate for the time being, he fills the gap with imaginary short-cuts. That is the *raison d'etre* of stories of miracles in our folk-lore, and of such fancies in our more sophisticated literature as flying carpets and flying horses in the *Arabian Nights* and the hundred and one tricks of Omar the Wily in the *Dastan-i-Amir Hamza*. In the *Talism-i-Hoshruba*, probably the longest yarn ever spun by a story teller, Afrasayab Jadu, the chief sorcerer and villain of the story, throws a magic explosive at his enemies, which not only makes short work of them, but destroys heaven and earth at the same time. I guess that Ahmad Husain Jah, the author, was imagining something akin to the atom bomb as it might be a few decades hence—if indeed, we on this little globe of ours are allowed to last that long. As regards Wells and Verne, the quick trip round the world, the journey to the moon (incidentally, this particular idea is as old as Cyrano de Bergerac — the original one that is, not Rostand's hero) and many other ideas, with which we are now familiar, were put forward first as scientific fiction. H. G. Wells has spoken of a stage of human development when, instead of s p e a k i n g to each other, men will 'think to' each other. Although such a development would be less than paradise to our speakers and writers (not to mention publishers !) there may come a day, for better or for worse, when Wells' prophecy might reach its threatened fulfilment.

You find this kind of prophetic forecasts of scientific events even in unsuspected quarters. Syed Insha, the courtier-poet of Saadat Ali Khan, the Nawab Wazir of Oudh in the eighteenth century, wrote an ode in honour of George III of Great Britain in the course of which he praised the royal horse (without seeing him, of course !) in the following terms:

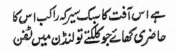

So fleet of foot is he that his rider
Has breakfast in Calcutta, and tiffin in London.

It looks as though Syed Insha, sitting in Lucknow two hundred years ago, was having visions of the jet age, of an age, indeed, which by present standards of speed, still lies in the future. Shakespeare's Puck went even further, when he declared his intention of setting 'a girdle round about the earth in eighty minutes'.

150

Alfred Tennyson, in his *Locksley Hall*, was much more specific. He spoke of 'pilots of the purple twilight dropping down with costly bales' which, though regarded as a mere flight of poetic fancy at the time, was a forecast of civil aviation. Tennyson also foresaw aerial warfare:

Saw the heavens filled with fighting,
                  and there was a ghastly dew,
From the nations' aery navies, grappling
                  in the purple blue.

That was decades ahead of time. Incidentally, when Monsieur Bleriot crossed the English Channel in 1909 by air, it is said that the English Customs thought that his aircraft should be assessed to duty on an ad hoc basis, as that kind of thing was not likely to happen again!

Has the progress of Science made Literature richer or poorer? Let us take English and Urdu. When we speak of 'dynamism', 'global,' 'streamlining', 'projection', 'atomic', 'explosive', 'science' or 'scientist', are we not borrowing from science? In Urdu we use words like

کیمیا' 'اضافی' 'جوہر' 'تجربہ' 'مشاہدہ' 'صیقل' 'فطرت' 'طبیعی' 'خلا'

and a whole host of others with a scientific origin, words which originally were the jargon of the scientists but have now become part of common speech. The poetry of Akbar Allahabadi is full of technical and scientific words which he introduced with humorous intention, but which are now as good Urdu as anything else.

Science is knowledge—systematized and rationalised knowledge. It has not only contributed words and expressions to literature but has also helped to make language more precise. Science does not gloss over facts or set them aside. It has to take account of them fully and accurately. One can say that accurate and exact descriptions in literature, particularly prose literature, are to a large extent, a reflection of the scientific spirit. The prose of W.H. Hudson, the famous naturalist, is an example, but there are others. The search for the right word, the exact word, which we see in writers like R.L. Stevenson, is akin to scientific discipline. On the other hand, we have examples of expressions which are quoted very often to illustrate a point of argument, but which seem to show ignorance of the fundamentals of science.

Take a familiar couplet, such as this:

خشت اول چوں نہد معمار کج
تا ثریا می رود دیوار کج

When the first brick laid by the builder is uneven,
The wall will never be straight even if it is raised to the stars.

Whatever the merits of this verse as poetry, the poet has certainly overlooked the fact that if the very first brick is not straight and level, it will not take more than a few more bricks on top of it for the whole lot to topple over, leave alone raising the wall to astral heights. Or let us take an Urdu verse which has won the approbation of no less an authority than Muhammad Husain Azad:

رشک آئینہ ہے اس رشک قمر کا پہلو
صاف ادھر سے نظر آتا ہے ادھر کا پہلو

My moon-like sweetheart is transparent like a mirror,
You look at her from this side and you clearly see the other.

In the first place, the poet has confused mirror with glass. A piece of glass is transparent while a mirror is not. Secondly, it looks as though only one side of the moon-like one is transparent; the other being obviously opaque. Were the other side also transparent, it would not be visible at all. What would be visible in that event would be the wall or some piece of furniture or whatever there may be on the other side of the sweetheart.

The great poetry of the world is based on observation of natural phenomenon and human behaviour. Let us take a verse of Kalim Kashani:

با من آویزش او الفت موج است و کنار
دمبدم با من و هر لحظہ گریزاں از من

My love, she loves me as the wave does love the shore;
She is drawn unto me each moment, and each moment draws away.

152

It is not an accurate description, and a beautiful one ?
Or the famous verse of Muhsin Taseer :

غریق قلزم وحدت دم از خودی نزند
بود محال کشیدن میان آب نفس

The one who is drowned in the Sea of Unity speaks not of Self;
You cannot draw breath when you are under water.
Or take a verse of Iqbal:

میانه من واورابط دیده و نظر است
که در نهایت دوری همیشه با اویم

Twixt her and me there is a bond as between the eye and its sight;
I am ever with her even when farthest away from her.
Or another verse of Iqbal:

از کاخ و کو جدا و پریشان به کاخ و کو
کردم بچشم ماه تماشای این سرای

I have seen this Carvanserai with the eye of the moon:
Which has its light diffused over streets and mansions,
and yet is apart from them.
Or the beautiful description of a fire-fly by Shelley :

Like a glow-worm golden
In a dell of dew
Scattering unbeholden
Its aerial hue,
Among the leaves and grass that screen it from the view.
Hassan bin Thabit, in one of his famous verses, has pointed to the
fundamental relationship between Art and Truth:

وان آشعر شعر انت قائله
شعر یقال از انشد ته صدقا

The best of thy poetry is that which, when recited,
Makes people say: 'He has told the truth'.

The classic example is that of the Arab poet who, when asked by a ruler to compose an ode in his honour, replied: "Let the Commander of the Faithful do something first and I shall write about it afterwards."

On the other hand, we have examples of gross exaggeration in poetry which may be admired as flights of fancy, but cannot be regarded as poetry in any real sense of the word. An example is the description by a Persian poet of a great army whose horses' hoofs raised so much dust that the seven earths were reduced to six and the seven heavens became eight (زمین شش شد و آسماں گشت هشت). Such fundamental disturbance of the structure of the Universe has neither happened nor is likely to happen at any time, least of all as a consequence of a cavalry operation. Poetry can be even more grotesque than this. The most pronounced example that comes to my mind is an Urdu couplet, of which (luckily for him !) I do not remember the author :

کیا نزاکت ہے کہ رخسار ان کے نیلے پڑ گئے
ہم نے تو بوسہ لیا تھا خواب میں تصویر کا

How delicate is my sweetheart !
Her cheeks turned blue
Even though I had kissed but her portrait,
And that too in a dream !
This hardly needs any comment.

If, out of regard for truth, a young man says to his sweetheart that he loves her, instead of saying, as he is likely to say in Urdu, that he is dying for love of her, I do not think it would jeopardise his chances of success. I am not suggesting that disappointed lovers do not commit suicide now and then, but it is also undeniable that most of them come away from the encounter with their hearts only slightly bruised, which they may nurse for just as long as they do not find other consolation. Edward Gibbon, when his father vetoed his romantic attachment, 'sighed like a lover, but obeyed like a son.' This happens to more people than are willing to make public confessions. Love and disappointments apart, exaggeration and inaccurate statement is the bane of literature and Urdu literature is full of it. Syed Ahmad Khan, with his Scientific Society, and the Nawab Shamsul Umara before him, sought to make Urdu a proper vehicle of precise and objective expression and thereby rendered a lasting service to Urdu language and literature.

In conclusion, it is clear that Science and Literature are not the antithesis of each other. There is no hostility between them, even though they spring from, and appeal to, different aspects of human nature. At the highest level, both of them owe their greatness to moments of inspiration, Literature being an act of creation, Science of discovery. They may exist together in the same man and may help rather than hinder each other. Science is the handmaiden of Truth. Art, too, must be based on Truth before it can ever become great Art. Science has made Literature rich and Literature can give Science an added perspective and purpose.

Whatever the popular impression—and I am thinking once again of our Arabic teacher who hated Science—Science and Literature are not two different ways of life or two opposite attitudes towards it. There is a possibility, in this age of specialization, when the sciences themselves have a tendency to go away from each other, that Literature and Science may come to a breaking point. That however is something that we should try to prevent at all costs. In the advanced countries of the world, there is a growing realization of the needs of the present situation, and educational syllabi are being revised to ensure that the students of science have an opportunity to imbibe the spirit of the humanities while students of the humanities are given basic training in science. This is an essential step towards the integration of the educational system and the personality of modern man.

We must have knowledge, truth, science. There must be more books on Science for the ordinary reader, the man in the street. It is important that men who are eminent in the literary field should turn to scientific writing. We have to bring Science into the home of every citizen of Pakistan, but we can never hope to do so unless we have books which are well written and can be read as Literature. Let there be more Science in Literature, and more Literature in Science.

155

INDEX

158

161